Make every day count.

Nora Prunty Briggs

Contents

Author's note

Making every day count is the key that has unlocked the shackles of blame, excuse, criticism, complaint and self-justification that have kept me imprisoned for years. Daily habits either work with you or against you and when they work for you; they silence the whinging in your head.

When I got to the stage that the stories in my head bored even me, the narrator I finally realised I had arrived at the place where 'enough was enough'. The self-limiting patterns of behaviours and beliefs had to go. I then accepted where I was at; accepted that 'this is me' without judgement. I began to work each day little by little towards an ungraded version of myself. I swapped criticism for self-compassion. It was then that I gave myself permission to rewire my factory settings. I started to reframe my past failures and mistakes as opportunities to reflect, learn and make course adjustments and not interpret them as flaws exclusive to myself; they were a sign of my humanity.

Our struggles are there to teach us, but only if we let them. Making every day count has helped me steer myself towards a better version of me. When you free yourself from the stories you keep telling yourself, then - and only then - can you create a shift that allows you to experience days that really count. This is very powerful. I am now less likely to dwell in the barren land of the 'shoulds' and 'if onlys'. Before this shift, my time and attention were hijacked by the myriad of distractions in today's world, my head chatter and the agenda of others. I was stuck! I now live my days with intention. Time is my most precious resource; once it's gone, I can't recreate it. I have reached the stage in my life where I don't want to waste any more time, any more days. I can't afford to, none of us can. Now, 'someday' gets replaced with today. Making every day count has allowed me to focus my mind on the things that are important to me and finally realise what is important to me. It feels as if the impossible has become possible; very much like it was with the younger version of myself.

Simple, doable daily habits are the magic elixir to making my days count and finally understanding how habits are created is the secret weapon to success. Start small and keep going. Each day is a privilege, and we need to make them count.

Living my life, making every day count has made me come alive. The world needs us all to come alive.

Dear Reader,

I feel very privileged that you have picked up my book and are flicking through the pages; finally deciding to read the introduction.

I have lost count of the number of times I have been in the exact same position as you are now; deliberating whether it is worth taking the time to read a book.

I have spent years trying to find an expert that could deliver a magical solution to my unanswered questions about health and wellbeing. In that time, I have read many great books, all with some little nugget of information or some wisdom that has inspired me and that I have attempted to integrate into my life. Those small changes have sparked a chain reaction and created a domino effect that has quietened the litany of 'shoulds' in my head as far as my health and wellbeing are concerned and how I live my days.

This book summarises my successes, my failures and the lessons that I have implemented from dipping into those books.

I have a quiet voice, and I'm not a risk-taker but when you feel you have something worth saying it's time to leap out of your comfort zone and speak a little louder and pray you have a soft landing on the other side. This book is my attempt to do that.

The truth is that there is no expert out there that can solve all your unanswered questions. In my experience it's when you decide to take the responsibility of becoming the expert on YOU - that's when you see real results.

Sometimes you will read a book that inspires you to make just one little change that sets in place a sequence of changes that are very powerful, as I did. If after reading this book, you make one small change in your life then I have achieved what I set out to do.

This book comes with a 'Repetition Warning'. There are places in the book that I have repeated myself because there are concepts that I want you to be fluent in by the time you put the book down. Repetition reinforces the strategy of 'intermittent reinforcement.' In other words, if you read an idea or concept enough times at some point, hopefully, it will become second nature and very comfortable.

My parents, not by word but with their deeds, instilled in me the desire that when I crossed paths with various people that I met in my life, that their lives should be all the better for having met me. After reading this book, I hope you have felt that our paths have crossed and that your life is better having done so.

Nora

By way of introduction

By the time I reach 50, which is fast approaching; I will have been around for 18,250 days; 11,680 days as an adult, 7,085 days married and 4,147 days as a Mum. The days have just flown by.

Shocking really; and I have let a lot of those days slip by.

For me that all changed in 2015. A combination of feeling overwhelmed by what the 'experts' were telling me about the way I should be leading the 'perfect life' and as a nutritional therapist, I too was supposed to be one of those so-called 'experts'. The frustration of my inability to put their suggestions and my own into consistent practice forced me to re-evaluate my whole approach to my physical and mental wellbeing. The catalyst to change came out of the blue.

Three ladies I knew quite well, one a very good friend, were diagnosed with cancer.

It only took one day for their lives to be changed forever.

I observed from the side-lines offering my support where I could, and watching as they moved forward with incredible courage and grace to meet this challenge. I remember at the time thinking how cruelly they had been swept without warning into hospital appointments, blood tests, prescription drugs, chemotherapy and radiotherapy sessions and, worst of all, the fear of facing the unknown. Their independence had been stripped away, and many choices and decisions were made for them by someone else. Their lives were thrust into the 'pause' mode - their future uncertain.

I remember trying to put myself in their position. I recall thinking about how I would cope if this happened to me. Who knows? Back then my thoughts were that it is much easier to 'Be ready' than 'Get ready' so that you hopefully would be able to summon up the resilience to cope with whatever your illness throws at you.

Cancer does not respect age, gender or race, and during my pharmacy career I have seen even the healthiest of people fall victim to this cruel disease. My conclusion was that right now I 'get' to get up each day and make my own choices, to decide what I want to do with my precious time - and indeed it was precious.

I wanted to appreciate this freedom I had. One thing I knew for sure, I didn't want to waste any more of my days. I wanted to become the best version of myself. In fact, I owed it to my three friends to live every day, making the best choices I could. So this is where I got my inspiration 'Make Every Day Count', where my goal was that on most nights that when I went to bed, I felt reassured that I had given my best to myself and my family. Focusing on changing my mindset and simplifying my life, together with the fundamentals of sleeping, eating, moving and resting seemed to me to be a good starting point incorporating 'the Goldilocks Effect' - just the right dose, not too much and not too little.

Getting to know myself, finding my purpose and honouring my values resonated with me too. I needed to know this so I could figure out where I wanted my days to take me. After all, a skipper never sets sail without plotting a course. I knew I wanted to 'create' my days rather than react to the chaos of them.

Over the last twelve months, I have been reminded of making every day count once again; to live every day, bringing the best version of myself to it. My Dad is in the late stages of dementia, and as I write this, he no longer knows who I am or for that matter any member of our family. He was diagnosed with the early stages of dementia at 79. He was still working full time and retired at 80.

On his 80th birthday he quietly announced to the family that he was going to write his memoirs; four years later he self-published his book through sheer grit, courage and determination. His short term memory was fading fast, and he was preciously holding on to his long term memory as long as he could. It is now a wonderful treasure that he has created for us, for my boys, their children, his friends and for future generations. Now, when I turn the pages of his book, I am witness to the outcome of his days that when strung together created a life well-lived.

According to Tom Rath, the writer of 'Eat, Move, Sleep', we have about 500 million moments in our life if one moment is to be defined as 3 seconds. It only takes a moment for your life to be changed with a diagnosis. It also only takes a moment to decide to change your life for the beter one day at a time. Let me help you make every day count and sew into them micro habits that concentrate on the five pillars of health and wellbeing – sleeping, eating moving, resting and simplifying your life which help to rewire your brain. Rewiring your brain enables you to sleep, eat, move and rest. Get these fundamentals right and anything is possible.

My friends' and my dad's experiences have inspired me to make sure I make my days really count.

About me

Me, age 7.

As many seven-year-olds do, I dreamt of having superpowers. Not extraordinary superpowers like fighting baddies or saving the planet, I just wanted ordinary 'superpowers' - I wanted to help people and make their lives easier. Over four decades later I hit a crisis, and I came to a very sudden and abrupt realisation...

I needed to figure out how to help myself first.

Hi, I'm Nora. I have immersed myself in the world of health and nutrition for almost 30 years.

First as a pharmacist and then as a nutritionist, I have dispensed endless potions, pills, magic bullets, tinkered with lots of food philosophies, stuffed myself with nutrition, health and wellbeing information. And I dare say I have helped a few people along the way. But for me, there has always been something missing.

I have ingested and digested an encyclopaedic amount of knowledge over the years but have ended up overwhelmed and totally frustrated. I almost had ended up on an obsessive crusade and was a martyr to the 'live well' campaign. I had created such a gap between what I knew and what I did that I had lost my mojo. I wanted and more importantly, needed to lighten up and enjoy my life again, so I threw it all up in the air and started with a clean slate. I went back to the basics.

The minimum effective dose of a drug was a concept I learned in my early pharmacy career. It's the sweet spot where a drug works but there are no toxic effects. Too little of a particular drug, it has no effect and too much of a particular drug then it becomes toxic. There is with every drug - a minimum effective dose, and that's what I wanted to experiment within my own lifestyle. I now refer to it as 'The Goldilocks Effect' of sleeping, eating, moving, resting and simplifying my life, getting it just right without the unwanted effects.

Potty training, bedtime routines, toddler tantrums, mastering times tables, and raising twin boys along with a couple of my favourite quotes by Mr Einstein and Mr Aristotle bizarrely revealed the missing pieces of the 'live well' puzzle for me.

Thinking differently, understanding habit formation, going back to the basics, incorporating the Goldilocks Effect together with a huge dose of perseverance (gained as a twin parent) unlocked the puzzle for me.

In the last three years I have done a complete U-turn, closed the nutrition books, the diet books, the fitness books and switched to reading books on the brain, willpower, habit formation, compassion, business and leadership in an attempt to get to the nitty-gritty of what actually goes on inside of my head.

Luckily for me, the research of what goes on in your head has exploded within the last decade. Neuroscientists are now really lifting the lid and understanding what is actually happening within the brain. Through trial and lots of error I began to think differently, introduce new habits into my daily life and slowly began to create sustainable changes in my life and at last 'live well with mojo intact.'

In a nutshell, I gingerly managed to cross the knowing/doing gap with baby steps.

Common knowledge (and believe me, we all have this knowledge within) is a wisdom that has been handed down through the generations on how to live well.

We have disregarded this wisdom in favour of the marketing hype and the shiny 'quick fix' mentality. We look to food scientists to tell us what to eat and consume foods that were made in a plant not from a plant as Michael Pollen highlights in his book Food Rules: An Eaters Manual.

It has taken me over four decades to figure out 'how to help myself' and looking back I now see that none of that time has been wasted. Change and transformation is a complicated process. I feel I am now in a position to help you with your transformation and help speed up the process so you don't have to make the same mistakes I did.

I want to give you peace of mind so that you can focus on the other important areas of your life where you can continually add value to your family and friends and, more importantly, add value to your own life.

To live a life worth living that is an example to those you live with and care for.

Creating a day full of micro-habits ticked many of the little 'should' gremlins in my head unlocking the key to living well.

Rewiring my brain by changing my mindset to think differently and making small changes in my sleeping, eating moving, resting and simplifying my life in equal measures with all areas holding equal importance helped me achieve results I had not thought possible. The intensity of my life that was permanently future-focused was replaced with a calmer, quieter, being more present, with a more consistent approach.

Lastly, when I look back on my seven-year-old self, I realise that we all possess our own set of superpowers to change our lives. We just need someone to give us a helping hand in discovering them.

Let that be me!

Know Thyself

(.....and while you are at it; your husband, your wife, your children, your relatives, your friends and your co-workers.)

Truthfully, being a Mum is the scariest thing I have ever embarked upon.

We were ecstatic at the initial ultrasound when it was first discovered that twins were on their way. At that point, I can say I entered 'fantasy land' merrily thinking of the combinations of genders and names that I would call the twins when they were born. I was clueless! Two little people and I would be responsible for them; yes, little old me!

At times, the sheer weight of the responsibility of bringing them up was (and is) overwhelming. But all I can do is 'my best', which I hope is good enough. To do my best, I must strive to be my best. That starts with taking responsibility for me, and that starts with knowing me.

Alas, the boys have taught me more than any O'Level (I wish I could say GCSE), A'Level, degree or any postgraduate qualification I have obtained, and they continue to do so.

Bringing up T&J is like having a minute-to-minute social experiment going on right in front of my eyes. They are non-identical twins and are very much chalk and cheese. Understanding this has helped me celebrate their uniqueness and help sort out the quarrels a little quicker between us all.

Do you know that eternal debate about 'nature and nurture"? In my opinion, without a doubt; NATURE IS VERY STRONG; VERY!!

From the moment - and I mean the very moment - the boys appeared, they were totally different. Their approach and responses to the outside world, life, school, and their interactions with their friends were and still are the polar opposite, and this has really kept me on my toes. It has taught me so much about them, myself and others.

They can hear or read the same information and respond very differently. Neither response is wrong. It's just them being themselves.

Over the years and with experience, I have had to develop two different styles of parenting to make sure I meet their needs dare I say it took me a while, and I will continue to learn. Being a Mum is an infinity project. Twin parenting has definitely brought home to me the message that one size does not fit all.

As you continue to read through these pages, I wanted to share some resources that I happened to stumble upon that really helped me figure out myself, my values, what's really important to me and my unique approach to life, friends, work etc. Basically, how I interact with the world around me. I hope it adds value to you too.

I must confess I have had no training in psychometric testing (scientific methods used to measure an individuals' behavioural style, personality and mental capabilities) so I am going to steer you towards some 'free quizzes' and the experts online that I really got value from that helped me understand myself a little better so that I could be aware of ways in which my behaviour and personality helps, hinders or even sabotages my efforts to make changes in my life and be the best version of me.

The quizzes and workbook are FUN to do too, and you get immediate feedback.

You might be surprised at the results. Some of you may have completed similar tests in your work environment but never translated them to your everyday life.

Have a go, I hope you will not be disappointed.

The following links will bring you to the quizzes:-

1.) The 16 personalities Test (127 million people have taken this test, maybe you have already done it, and I was late to the party) www.16personalities.com

2.) I have spent years trying to uncover my core values. Without a doubt, when I accidentally came across Dawn Barclay and her wonderful website Living Moxie at dawnbarclay.com, my search was over. On her site, one of her resources is 'The Core Values Workbook' - is incredible and FREE.

In her own words, Dawn introduces; 'The Core Values Workbook' as follows 'Does it feel like you don't know who you are anymore? Do you want to understand yourself better? Frustrated you don't know what's next for you? You've done living the scripts belonging to others. The prospect of knowing your core values - now - is an amazing discovery. It's a great piece of self-knowledge to have for life, career, and business. Knowing what you stand for so you can make choices that well, make sense, to give your life a purpose and direction, intentionally moving towards your goals, and heck, this one knowing who you really are, it's big stuff. It's also a challenge. The Core Values workbook - a free resource - will help.'

3.) a) Gretchen Rubin's Quiz: The Four Tendencies www.surveygizmo.com/s3/4232520/gretchenrubinfourtendenciesquiz

b) I have included a link below to a blog post that Gretchen wrote about New Year's Resolutions. I hope it all makes sense when you read through it and find your particular tendency. Any new habit or changes in your life can replace the words "New Year's Resolutions" when you are reading through it. https://gretchenrubin.com/2017/12/four-tendencies-newyearsresolutions

In summary my understanding of the four tendencies is that in order to make changes; the Obligers out there need accountability, the Questioners need to find some way of getting over their 'analysis-paralysis', Upholders – you can do it under your own steam, you just need some sound information and the Rebels among you, you have to have total autonomy, it has to be your decision. You are never going to follow the crowd, so I hope you came across my work all by yourself and no one recommended it.

Lastly, to end this section, I wanted to add a personal note about one of the findings I uncovered doing the personality test and quite possibly more to do with my understanding of that particular personality trait. I am very much in the INTROVERT CAMP. This really shocks people when I tell them. They almost sympathise with me with words like "no -

you couldn't be an introvert!" as if it's an affliction and I've lost out on the personality lottery.

In the past, when I have thought of 'introverts', I too have thought their main characteristics were shyness or timidness. For the majority of the time, I am so not that way, BUT there are times that I am. I had completely misunderstood what it meant to be an introvert. Now I know that I top up my MOJO from within. Extroverts top up their mojo from being around other people, externally. They need other people. Don't get me wrong I can be the life and soul of the party, in fact if you were having a party I would probably be at the top of your invite list. But for me, large gatherings can almost be too much sometimes. I need to get to the party and connect with one or two people. If I pack too much into my life, I get overwhelmed. There are times when I need 'stillness'!

Another interesting observation – again, I'm sorry - the boys. One of the boys is an Extrovert and the other an Introvert. Didn't I say they were polar opposites? It's fun in my house. Anyway when they misbehaved as toddlers and the 'naughty step' was the recommended solution by the gurus at that time; my introverted son was only too delighted to spend time by himself, and he could calm himself down very quickly when he was put on it.

As for my little extroverted son, it was complete torture. This exclusion time in his eyes did not match the crime. I might as well have sent him to outer Siberia with just his nappy on. It took me a while, but when I did figure out the personality difference, the naughty step as a means of changing behaviour was swiftly abandoned. The book 'The Power of Introverts' written by Susan Cain, has really added to my life. It showed me that there is a place for 'little ole me' in a very extroverted world. I have provided a link to her TED talk below for those other introverts out there... enjoy!

Nearly 20 million people have watched this TED talk 'The Power of Introverts'.

www.ted.com/talks/susan_cain_the_power_of_introverts

And finally, if anything I have written inspires you to make changes in your life, and I hope it has - my underlying message is to be you & really get to know you, start with where you're at and switch criticism for compassion.

So what legacy do you want to leave your children, your children's children and future generations?

A 200ml amber bottle of magic elixir and a strawberry flavoured Chupa Chup lolly dispensed by Mr O'Neill, our local pharmacist, was the catalyst for my pharmacy career.

At seven, I suffered from repeated bouts of tonsillitis. Even to this day I can still remember the pain. Within twenty-four hours of starting the medicine, I would soon begin to feel better.

My hero at the time was my local pharmacist (or chemist as they were known in those days). No credit was given to our family doctor because the route to my recovery included being on the receiving end of a very painful intramuscular injection in a very delicate part of my anatomy - my bum; the pain of which was almost as memorable as the sore throat. SO in my seven-year-old mind as far as I was concerned the pharmacist had the cure to all ills!

In 1992 I started my career as a basic grade pharmacist in the NHS in a hospital on the Wirral. I worked with three phenomenal principal pharmacists, the three amigos - Keith, Don and John. They were innovative, enthusiastic and very patient and staff-focused. And they all had high hopes for me. I had other plans.

I had just graduated with a First in Pharmacy, and within a year of working there I had published my first research paper in an International medical journal based on my undergraduate research entitled 'Does anyone know what medication the patient should be taking?' It's still relevant today. I had spent the previous five years focused on becoming a pharmacist. I'm not the smartest cookie in the jar, but I am not afraid of hard work, and I love to learn. I always had that inner belief that 'I'm going to do this'. In doing so, I had burnt myself out, and I wanted a bit more life experience to add to my CV, so I packed my pharmacy degree in my rucksack and went travelling. I finally landed in Australia to work in Wilson's Pharmacy, which matched my experience on the Wirral.

Pharmacy has been very good to me, and I have never lost that deep down feeling of wanting to help others, I just wasn't sure working either in community or hospital pharmacy was the way to achieve that. Don't get me wrong, I have a lot of admiration for the NHS and have met some terrific people that have inspired me, and I have had to avail of treatment for myself down through the years, but the NHS is struggling, which we are all too aware.

A report published on April 5th 2015 on the long term sustainability of the NHS and adult social care in the UK was the outcome of a year-long inquiry by a House of Lords Select Committee, chaired by the crossbench peer and obstetrician Narendra Patel. The Committee's main conclusion was that unless several changes are implemented, the NHS and adult social care system will be unsustainable. I recently read a great article in the Lancet that was published in April 2017 that summarised the report, and it makes very interesting reading. Here are a few conclusions that I have pulled out for your attention and included a few of my own:

There are many reasons why the NHS is struggling; the UK's ageing population is certainly a big factor, and it's one that all health systems in the world are struggling with. If you take a peek at future demographic changes it is quite alarming! Of particular significance is that all over the world, people are living longer and having fewer children, very soon the fastest-growing segment of the population will be over 65's. All countries will need bold healthcare and social policies to cope with these demographic changes.

In Europe, the decline in the working-age population will be particularly acute. For every four working-age people per elderly person in 2015, there'll be just two in 2050. (An ageing population will require greater spending on healthcare.)

- Medical advances have meant that people are living longer, as mentioned above.

When the NHS was created, life expectancy was 13 years shorter than it is now.

This is something to celebrate! Infectious diseases are no longer a significant threat, and heart attacks do not claim the lives of people early in the same numbers. Even cancer is not the death sentence it once was - half of people now survive for a decade or more. But this progress has come at a cost. People are living with a growing number of long term chronic conditions - diabetes, heart disease and dementia. The NHS was designed to treat acute illness and has poorly adapted to managing chronic disease. These are more about care than cure - what patients usually need is support. Although increased longevity of life was one of the triumphs of the 20th century, the challenge for today is to ensure that those years are healthy years.

By the age of 65, most people will live with at least one of these illnesses. By 75 they will have two.

• Care for older people costs much more. The average 65-year-old costs the NHS 2.5 times more than average 30-year-old. An 85-year-old costs more than five times as much.

• Other recommendations of the report were that the NHS constitution should be redrafted to make it clear that access to NHS involves responsibilities as well as rights for patients, and that the population have a 'common duty' to live healthily to support the sustainability of the NHS.

• There is still widespread dissatisfaction with the prevention agenda. There is a long-awaited ambition to move from an 'illness' to a 'wellness' service. Preventative care must take priority. To add to these worries:

◦ Failure of GP recruitment to keep pace with demand is set to leave a shortfall of 9,940 GPs across the UK by 2020.

◦ Retention of GPs is also a problem. The College has identified 594 practices across the UK where 75% of the GPs are aged 55 and over— with the retirement of so many GPs is a present danger for these practices; the College has identified them as being at risk of closure by 2020. Nationwide, the proportion of GPs aged 55 or over in 2015 was 20.8% in England, 19.9% in Scotland, 23% in Wales and 25.2% in Northern Ireland.

So if we don't take care of ourselves, who is going to take care of us?

Halfway through this century, I will be in my 80's, my boys will be grown men in their 40's, and if I am lucky enough, I may be a grandmother.

I came to the parenting party late, so if I want to see my grandchildren, I need to invest all my efforts now, and I owe it to my children. In my eighties, I want to be fit, healthy and full of vitality. I want to see my children pass on to their children the habits that they saw their mum use throughout her life, that they were inspired to follow because I integrated them seamlessly (almost) into my day. I don't want to leave them with a legacy of the 'shiny new object' approach to their health where the media dictate the next new health craze; marketed in the background by a consumable product or a streamable digital product or even an airbrushed model, the picture of fake health. I want them to follow a set of habits that have stood the test of time and are immune to age, gender, creed or culture and come with no expiry date.

Habits they saw their mother live by.

I have created all my rituals with the 80-year-old me in mind. I know only too well as I have outlined above that the NHS will not be able to unravel the damage of an unhealthy lifestyle followed by me.

And as my cousin once said to me, Type 2 diabetes and dementia are in the post for us (thanks Gerald). That might well be so but I am going to hopefully return those chronic diseases to sender, address unknown because of the lifestyle I follow.

There are no guarantees but, if I fall under the chronic disease bus, I want to make sure I've tried my best to prevent this happening.

Lifestyle matters, and as Nobel Prize winner Elizabeth Blackburn wrote: "Genes load the gun, but environment (that includes your lifestyle) pulls the trigger." We can do very little about the genes we received. In fact, we were glad to get them (scientists estimate that the probability of you being born is 1 in 400 trillion!). We can, however, heavily influence the 'passing on' of a set of healthy lifestyle habits.

Our children, especially in their early years, will mimic our behaviours and will, therefore, have well chiselled neural circuits for these healthy lifestyle habits in their brains. DOING as a parent will far outweigh anything you SAY. You are contagious. By the time your children reach adulthood, they may have a constitutional responsibility to keep themselves healthy to counteract the effects of an ageing population. Through your efforts, they will be well prepared.

So what legacy do you want to leave your children, your children's children and future generations?

If we each live properly and create a set of daily healthy habits that can be handed down through the generations, a legacy worth passing on, collectively we will flourish.

The Key to Success: Understanding How Our Brain Works

Have you ever wondered why many of us are unable to stick to our New Year's resolutions? Eat healthily (whatever that means!), go to the gym three times a week, avoid chocolate, drink less, get to bed on time, zero inbox, complete that to-do list; the list goes on and on.

We take on far too many changes at the same time. I suffered with this battle plan in the past. I now call it 'The Bridget Jones approach'. You know, you wake up on New Year's Day, slightly hung-over, sleep-deprived with zero energy and you want your whole life to change within the next six weeks, but preferably instantly.

This is Mission Impossible.

We over-estimate what we can achieve in six weeks and underestimate what we can achieve in a year. It is impossible for the brain to make all these changes. Change is tough on the brain, very tough.

It might shock you, but your brain is fundamentally LAZY.

That's harsh! Surprised me too when I first read that. I had my brain down as all-knowing, all-doing and working at full pelt all the time for my benefit. It turns out its sole focus is making sure we survive and in the process, use as little precious mental energy as possible.

Change uses up a lot of valuable energy and any change no matter how small is interpreted in the brain as a threat. The brain cannot measure how big the threat is, and something very trivial can be catastrophised in our brain as something similar in scale to a 'nuclear threat'.

Inside your brain, there is a daily struggle between your emotional brain (the limbic system) and your thinking brain (the prefrontal cortex). It's that never-ending battle between the 'I want' and the tedious 'I must'.

Dan Siegel, world-renowned clinical professor of psychiatry, cleverly describes the inside of your brain as a house with an upstairs and downstairs. The downstairs represents the functions of the emotional brain (the limbic system). Its focus is on keeping us safe and making sure our needs are met. Downstairs are where our habits (good or bad) are coded, saved, and our impulses dwell. Our instinct for survival originates here.

Downstairs looks out for danger, sounds the alarm and makes sure we are ready to fight, run, freeze or hide when we are faced with danger.

The upstairs is your thinking brain (prefrontal cortex). This is where all the planning, decision making, emotional regulation (where we think about our feelings), creative genius and flexibility takes place and here resides your WILLPOWER.

When we focus, we are using our thinking brain. Our brains work best when the upstairs and the downstairs work together. There are times when the upstairs (thinking brain - prefrontal cortex) decides we MUST at any cost make changes to our behaviours often around January 1st. The downstairs - the emotional limbic system - on the other hand, sees these changes as a massive threat that will compromise our safety and ultimately our survival.

The downstairs doesn't want to play and throws its toys out of the bathwater.

Now the upstairs can take matters into its own hands and enforce its decision by using 'WILLPOWER', but this is a valuable resource that demands a lot of mental energy. There are a lot of demands on the upstairs apart from willpower so our willpower can get depleted very quickly, especially at times when we need it most. We do need to use willpower initially when changing our behaviour, but then we hope and pray that the downstairs comes on board and starts converting these new behaviours that have been repeated numerous times into Habits.

With the 'Bridget Jones approach,' we are setting ourselves up for abysmal failure. Yes, you can keep going on with gritted teeth and willpower for the first few days, even for a week or two, but soon your initial inspiration, motivation and resolve have expired. Upstairs and downstairs are suffering from miscommunication.

To make changes in our lives, we need effective communication and collaboration between the upstairs of our brain and the downstairs. We have to build a solid set of stairs which allows messages to flow freely between them.

As mentioned earlier, the downstairs is very, very stubborn to change. If it gets any hint of change or hasn't given its full approval to a change, it goes into lockdown, and any decision or new change enforced by the upstairs is immediately thrown into the bin.

Let's look at the downstairs in a little more detail. As I mentioned earlier the areas in the brain responsible for habits the basal ganglia (Base- Al Gang-Lia) and impulses, the nucleus accumbens (New- Clee -Us- A- Come-Benz) are found in the downstairs part of the brain. Our habits are our default operating mode and use very little brain energy. The brain is happiest in this state. Our impulses are there so we can experience pleasure, thank goodness! Sex and food mean we reproduce and we thrive; essential to our survival. Habits and impulses work via dopamine release - our reward neurotransmitter. When habits are forming, dopamine release is necessary to keep us repeating an enjoyable sequence of steps so that they become encoded and automatic.

We repeat what feels good. Acting on our impulses releases a huge amount of dopamine, and again this feels good, very good. Our nucleus accumbens is so efficient at seeking out pleasure that after a while, dopamine is released in anticipation of the pleasure. Once formed, your impulses are very hard to fight.

Once I understood the upstairs/ downstairs concept of the brain, it was like I had full absolution for any previous failed attempts at making changes in my life before that point. This was literally like my 'get out of jail free card'. So it hadn't been my fault, my previous failed attempts. I just hadn't fully understood how the brain worked.

The next step is for the upstairs and downstairs parts of our brains to fully co-operate with each other to change our behaviour, our habits and reach our goals.

Let the story begin…

Keeping your Brain in Order, Keeping your House in order.

Toy Story, Nanny McPhee, Paddington, and Jungle Book: I love them all.

One of the best bits of being a Mum is that I get to go to the cinema and watch movies with the boys (purely for their benefit I might add). I have even made the boys go to "Cinderella" and "Beauty and the Beast". Top of my list is the Pixar Movie, "Inside-Out" released in 2015. It tells the story of Riley a happy, hockey-loving 11-year-old girl. Her world turns upside down when her family have to move to San Francisco. Riley's emotions are portrayed as characters within her head with unique traits and personalities. The film cleverly tells the story of how her characters (emotions) interact as she tries to deal with this stressful situation. I am going to borrow a little piece of Pixar's magic.

Now I have to declare that I am not a psychologist and definitely not a neuroscientist (though I do have a neuroscience certificate). For as long as I can remember, I too have always made any scientific information a bit playful.

I have had to find the fun aspect of anything I have studied in order to learn it, remember it and answer exam questions on it. I have converted horrendous biochemical pathways, the mind-boggling anatomy and physiology of the body, mode of action of drugs, multiple detox pathways in the liver, the list goes on and created really ridiculous characters or mnemonics so that I can bring an element of fun to the task.

This is purely my adaption - of Dan Siegel's - brain model. I have added imaginative characters to the upstairs and downstairs of the house as a child would in a similar fashion to a dolls house. This is how I have added my own spin to it, so it makes sense to me.

Downstairs: The Emotional Brain

So, let me introduce you to the characters that I imagine living in the downstairs part of my brain (and maybe live in yours).

Our emotional brain, the limbic system firmly resides downstairs. Its principal function is 'self- preservation', and many characters make up this system. In some way, it's like our 'emotional switchboard'. The characters are in no particular order;

Sergeant Major Amygdala (A- Mig-Dal-A) - at your service.

I imagine the Amygdala kitted out in army fatigues ready for action at the first whiff of danger.

Fortunately, he has kept us alive since time began in some very precarious and life-threatening situations.

But modern living and modern stresses have allowed Sergeant Major Amygdala to become overly sensitive.

He becomes trigger happy, which completely shuts down Mr PFC – the thinking part of the brain. I'll introduce you to him a little later. When things get way out of hand Sergeant Major Amygdala can totally blow his gasket, and we suffer from 'AN AMYGDALA HIJACK'. This is the equivalent of a toddler having a tantrum. As adults, we may not display the outward signs of a tantrum but believe me it's all going on inside our heads.

It's those times in our lives when we have become emotional, and reason has gone out the window, and we become emotionally paralysed.

We are incapable of making a decision, even a simple one. Have you ever found yourself in this situation? There are strategies that keep Sergeant Amygdala in check, but for now, just being aware of him is good enough.

Party Animal Nucleus Accumbens (New-Clee- A- Come-Benz) is only interested in having a good time. Pleasure is her ultimate goal, and she LOVES getting her fix of dopamine - the reward chemical. The more dopamine she gets, the more she wants. This party animal bounces from one impulse to the next. Marketing and advertising departments are always looking for novel ways of inviting our Nucleus Accumbens to the party. And on a side note somewhere in a laboratory, a Food Scientist is conjuring up the best combination of sugar and fat (the bliss point) that will light up our Nucleus Accumbens like a firework display that ensures our need for their product and maximises their sales.

Director of Status Quo - Madam Hypothalamus (Hi -Po-Thal-Mus) loves keeping the status quo within the body.

Madame Status Quo is on constant vigilance to see if we are under any type of threat. She can switch on our flight or fright (sympathetic nervous system) in case of danger and switch on our 'rest and digest (parasympathetic nervous system) when all around us is calm. Yes, as you may have guessed Madam Hypothalamus is more often than not got her finger pressed firmly on our 'flight or fright' switch.

Ole' Captain Basal Ganglia (Base-Al-Gang-Lee-A) – he has been around forever and forever.

He's responsible for putting the 'auto' into 'autopilot'.

He encodes new behaviours, whether good or bad into habits and he loves, loves, loves repetition, repetition, and repetition. His age-old advice to us would be practice, practice, practice your new behaviour and reward yourself every time you do it (give yourself a high five or shout "I did it") because every time you do that he gets a wee hit of dopamine. Repetition, repetition is the name of the game, and he is only too happy to convert our repeated behaviour into a 'shiny ole habit.'

The other reason that Ole' Captain Basal Ganglia loves practice is that it causes myelination. Myelination takes place when myelin, a fatty substance is laid down along the neurons (nerve cells) when we repeat and practice a particular behaviour. Myelin acts as an insulating material and speeds up the transmission of impulses along these neurons so that before we know it, repeated behaviour has its very own neural pathway in the brain and has become automatic and a habit. Bingo!

Once 'Ole Captain Basal Ganglia' knows we are serious about a new behaviour, as we have practiced it so many times that even he has got the message and more than enough dopamine has been released. It is then that he firmly superglues these behaviours as a habit into our brains. I can imagine at this stage 'Ole Captain Basal Ganglia' casually saying to Mr.PFC 'the pressure's off now MR.PFC, I have this one covered so there is no need to use your precious willpower anymore. It's time to get on with some more pressing issues'. There's possibly a hint of a smug grin on his wrinkled, weather beaten face. And he has a right to be smug. Habits are the default mode of the brain and use up very little mental energy.

There it is; all the characters that I imagine living in the downstairs part of your head and their names. I hope you found that useful in making this topic a little more accessible. I always pause and think of these characters when I am struggling with a change in my life. I have strategies up my sleeve that I employ when my emotional system has taken over, and I will share these in later chapters.

Upstairs: The thinking brain

Now, let's take a tour UPSTAIRS – the Prefrontal Cortex remembering that the only way we gain access to the upstairs is when the downstairs (emotional limbic system) is on-board.

The main character and leading role is played by Mr Prefrontal Cortex - Mr PFC (the thinking brain) I imagine he's like the headmaster of a very large school. He's very dapper, suited and booted.

He wears very thick-rimmed glasses, and he has a tough job. He's always got our best interests at heart. He thinks we are unstoppable. He is focused, continually paying attention, planning, making decisions and goal-driven so that we move forward in a positive way. He wants us to thrive. He's also responsible for that precious resource; Willpower, our self-control. If we took away our prefrontal cortex, we would be ruled by our desires and impulses. This would result in reduced ability to plan for the future or think about the consequences of our actions.

The only drawback of MR PFC is that he uses up a lot of energy. He's a bit like your smartphone charge. If you have had a restful sleep, Mr PFC is topped up full of energy and ready to go first thing in the morning. But then the chaos of our day starts, and we start having to make DECISIONS.

According to the latest research, we have to make, on average, 35,000 decisions per day. Most are mundane, and we are often making the same decision over and over again, and we are totally oblivious to it. Will I get out of bed now or put on the snooze button? What am I going to have for breakfast? What will I wear today? Will I take my umbrella? What will I do this weekend? And it goes on and on. Mr PFC patiently decides for us, but in the process drains his battery. If his battery is drained, I'm afraid there's no energy left to redirect to our willpower and our self-control evaporates.

Think about this; when are we most likely to break our new year's resolutions? First thing in the morning or late in the evening? By evening time we are suffering from 'DECISION FATIGUE.' We can help Mr PFC do an effective job if we use a strategy of DECIDING IN ADVANCE.

You may not be aware of this, but we have seen this in action on more than one occasion. During his Presidency, Barrack Obama wore multiple copies of the same outfits, as did Steve Jobs. They were cleverly reducing the number of daily decisions they had to make. A lot of successful people accomplished some of their greatest work first thing in the morning before their Mr PFC has become utterly depleted.

More importantly, it is worth mentioning again if we have an overwrought emotional system (downstairs) Mr PFC becomes totally inaccessible, and the door to the Headmasters Office is very firmly locked.

SOS (save our skins) and Feel Good Neurochemistry.

Our brains, as mentioned above, are hardwired to expect the worst so that historically we were able to survive. We are now living in a digital age, but our brain's chemistry is stuck in caveman times. Back then, two things were top of the 'to do' list - to survive and experience pleasure. After all, we needed to be around to pass on our valuable genes. It was the 'era' of Survival of the Fittest so if you survived your genes were indeed valuable. Then, it made sense to be alert to danger and expect bad things to happen at around every boulder.

Experiencing pleasure gave us something to look forward to after the survival business was all taken care of.

When we expect bad things to happen, that sense of danger or we feel stress, Madame Hypothalamus our Status Quo director immediately floods our body with adrenaline and cortisol. These are our self-preservation hormones; they speed up and create the hyper-alert state, which allows us to react our way out of danger rapidly. Their intentions are good, but they overstay their welcome, especially cortisol. Our modern equivalent caveman's stressors are being late for work, missing the train, forgetting to pack little Johnnies rugby kit, red lights, figuring what's for dinner at 5pm and finding nothing in the fridge; these are our modern-day sabre-toothed tigers. Our bodies are running in top gear and using up our resources fast and we literally become worn out, one little stressor at a time. Regrettably, our 'get us away from danger systems' in our body cannot differentiate between a big stressor and a little stressor.

Feel Good Neurotransmitters

Feel good neurochemistry; to counteract cortisol, our stress hormone, our brains have several chemicals to make us feel good. My favourites are Dopamine, Serotonin and Oxytocin.

Dopamine - we get little shots of dopamine release when we get things done. It exists in our brains to make sure we achieve our goals. Habits are fuelled by dopamine. Dopamine doesn't really differentiate between little goals and big goals so we can get maximum advantage from this by creating micro-goals, micro wins/ successes, so we get our little squirt of dopamine to keep us going.

Serotonin - most people have heard of serotonin the happy chemical which lifts our mood, but I think it is much more than that. It's the 'I did a good job today, and I'm proud of myself' hormone. We also get it when we get recognition from other people too, and it feels really, really good. It's almost the opposing effect of dopamine; dopamine spurs you on. In contrast, serotonin gives you that quiet, calm, satisfying feeling when you're modestly proud of yourself. For me making sure we are balancing dopamine (wow, I've done it!) and serotonin (I am proud of what I did, and I feel great about it) is really important. Too much dopamine and we are continually on the lookout for the next best thing, very future-focused and never satisfied. Serotonin is more about the here and now. It's the appreciation hormone.

Oxytocin is by far, my favourite. My boys are well versed in how to increase Oxytocin. It's the cuddle hormone that gives you that warm, fuzzy feeling. It's the antidote to cortisol. Get the benefits for yourself. Give someone a hug and hold that hug for 20 seconds. Acts of kindness also release this hormone. Take, for example, petting your dog, both the giver and receiver gain the benefits. It's a very generous hormone.

Understanding the characters and the parts that they play in our brain really helps when we are struggling or when we want to make important shifts in our life. Having an insight into neurotransmitters really helps too. Making every day Count which integrates the pillars of health; sleeping, eating, moving, resting and simplifying life can support the characters in your brain to rewire your brain and rewiring can help with your sleeping, eating, moving, resting and simplifying your life. It's a win-win!

The Upstairs/Downstairs Model

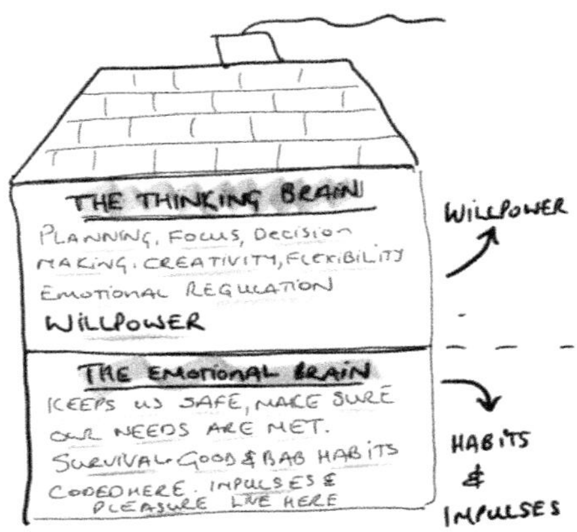

Understanding Habits

Daily habits matter the most because they add up to create our life. We are a product of what we do daily; getting up in the morning, showering, getting dressed, the school run or commute, the list goes on habits, habits, habits. In order to make every day count, we need to focus on our current habits. Replacing old habits with upgraded versions and adopting new habits that add value to our days and ultimately our lives.

Habits, whether good or bad, are powerful. They are hotwired and hardwired into our brain. Ole Captain Basal Ganglia has happily helped us get to this point.

The good news is that it's a lot easier to create new habits and replace redundant habits when we understand how habits are formed in the first place. Habits are the magic ingredient to making consistent, positive changes in our lives.

The dilemma that many of us face when we want to make seismic changes in our life is when we are seduced by the 'Bridget Jones' approach. This is to change everything, starting straight away, immediate results, please! NOW! Inevitably at some point, the downstairs characters will go into an emotional spin and make a fast retreat to their comfort zone; our ineffective default behaviours. We are left frustrated with yet another failed attempt at making changes to our lives. Back in default mode yet again which feels familiar, safe, where we are surviving but a long way from thriving.

Change feels uncomfortable. We are literally changing our biochemistry, neurochemistry and physiology. Understanding the nitty-gritty of habit formation is the secret sauce to success. Even before we make changes in our life, we need to be taught how to form a habit. It's a skill; like learning a musical instrument, a new sport. It takes time, effort, and practice. Once we learn the various stages of habit formation, we can apply the lessons learned to all areas of our life, big, small, trivial and enormous.

Many of us, when making changes in our life, can suffer from 'Genius Syndrome'. We decide to make a change or many changes in our lives and we launch ourselves, unaided, without a plan into the abyss. In theory, we think it should be easy. We are fuelled by a super surge of inspiration and enthusiasm, and we have that false sense of security that this time it's going to be different, this time we are going to do it. And yes it's possibly easy to do for a day or two maybe even six weeks until ....we hit a keystone date; that holiday, that wedding, that milestone birthday. After that, the struggle begins; the ability to consistently maintain these positive changes every day from here on in for the months and years to follow is too much. Just when we thought the victory was in sight; failure rears its ugly head, and we slip and slither down the big fat tortuous snake like that in Snakes and Ladders when we falsely think the end is in sight. We were doing so well, but now we find ourselves back at square one, and our initial inspiration, enthusiasm and optimism have perished. Once evaporated, these are extremely hard to conjure up again. We've all been there. We forget we are always a work in progress.

They say we can achieve anything in life once we put our minds to it.

I've heard this countless times. I now add a little addendum: - we can achieve anything in life once we put our minds to it provided we have created a set of appropriate habits.

The Habit Loop

There are some really clever 'habit gurus' that have dissected every step of habit formation. The likes of Charles Duhigg, Professor BJ Fogg and James Clear. If it was not for their work, I would still be going around in ever-decreasing circles probably still hankering after the 'perfect diet!'

They all agree that there is a 'Habit Loop'

Most of our days are spent in habit mode so it may be difficult to remember when a particular habit first got installed into our brain, but it was more than likely we created a 'Habit Loop'.

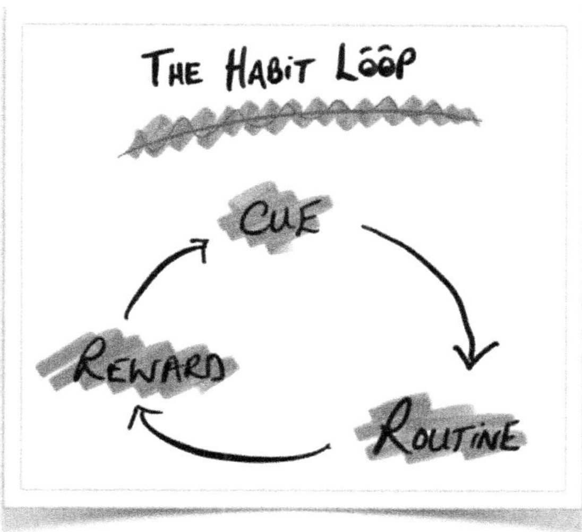

CUE ROUTINE REWARD

The 'cue' is the trigger that prompts us to start carrying out the steps of the habit. I find it really useful to think of it as a trigger, prompt, stimulus, an activation switch that is needed to give you that wake-up call to getting started. Cues can come in many forms - an alarm we have intentionally set, a particular feeling, a physical urge, the sight of something, even the moments after another habit is completed i.e. flossing after brushing your teeth, the sight of your running shoes, the sight of the fruit bowl on the kitchen table in plain view, the chocolate bar beside the tills, particular locations etc. The list goes on.

Just as a side note, many of our habits today were programmed in our childhood and our No.1 cues were our parents' voices who tirelessly reminded us to do the right thing. Does 'brush your teeth, tidy your room, finish your homework, sit properly and tie your shoelaces sound familiar? We now need to 'coach' ourselves to form habits by finding appropriate cues. Our parents were also our most influential role models. We copied their behaviours and their habits.

The cue is an extremely powerful part of the habit loop because our brains eventually will respond automatically to it. It takes a lot of effort to counteract our brains response; often, we are oblivious to the cues that have already been programmed into our behaviour. In this, the digital age, experts have focussed enormous energy on figuring out suitable cues to interrupt accidentally on purpose our daily routine. Think of the constant 'ping' of your smartphone or laptops, alerting us to text messages, emails, and calling us to action. We are trying to find a similar obvious cue that creates that momentary interruption to alert us to begin the 'routine' step of the habit. We need to make our cues obvious. Metaphorically speaking; we need to trip over them!

The body has about 11,000 sensory receptors. Approximately 10,000 are dedicated to sight - post-it notes strategically distributed throughout your environment are a fantastic aid in reminding us of our strategically chosen cue. We need all the help we can get. Alarms also make fantastic cues.

CUE - **ROUTINE** - REWARD

The ROUTINE is the actual steps or the sequence of actions that are the habit itself and its initiated after we have been prompted by our chosen cue. It's what we literally 'do'. Essentially we are trying to construct a new neural pathway in the brain. Scripting the routine by actually writing the steps down or speaking each step out loud might sound a tad silly, but it is really important. When we think through what we are going to do, we are automatically visualising ourselves doing it, and this really helps in laying down the foundations for the new neural pathway in the brain. Building new habits is like hacking through a new pathway in an overgrown jungle; lots of hard work is needed initially. Much easier mentally to take the path well-travelled; our old habits!

CUE - ROUTINE - **REWARD**

Though it might not seem obvious, every habit ends in a reward. Even brushing your teeth has a reward; the freshness you feel in your mouth.

If the reward is interpreted in some way as positive, your brain will remember what you did and want to repeat it. A reward can be anything, but most commonly, it is a feeling. Every time we reward ourselves after we have completed the routine part of the habit Ole Captain Basal Ganglia receives a little squirt of dopamine. Dopamine fuels the habit loop. Eventually, after looping the loop of the habit loop many times, cravings develop, and the loop becomes self-perpetuating, and the habit is formed.

When a habit loop isn't fuelled by a craving because it has not been practised enough, it requires a lot more effort to be established. If you don't normally exercise and go to the gym only a couple of times you'll most likely find it difficult to form a habit. This could be because Old Captian Basal Ganglia hasn't experienced any rewards worth craving. He needs a continual hit of dopamine.

The REWARD can be totally unique and suits our individual personality helping us acknowledge that 'we've done good' - pardon the grammar. This makes us want to repeat the experience again and again and AGAIN. The reward can take the form of a smile, an exaggerated victory dance, a yelp; any gesture or noise that we make that registers our success in completing the routine. In fact; the 'goofier' the better. The brain loves simplicity and goofiness. Have you seen professional sportspeople celebrate their successes? Especially footballers - that's what I mean by 'GOOFY!' The bigger the positive feeling that we can generate immediately after we have completed our new 'habit routine', the better our results. That's because we have created a more pronounced DOPAMINE DRIP. We want Ole Captain Basal Ganglia to be jumping around doing the dopamine dance. We really, really, REALLY need to acknowledge and exaggerate our successes.

We have become immune to our tiny successes because our inner critic has such a loud voice in our head. When was the last time you appreciated yourself? Once you experienced the rewards a number of times as mentioned; eventually, the brain starts to crave the routine that resulted in the reward. Very clever!

We have a new puppy in our house, Chloe, and every time she manages to peepee successfully outdoors the kids, and I are jumping for joy and lavishing plenty of praise on her. It is a perfect example of 'reward-based training'. Chloe is fast developing her 'outdoor habit' and thank goodness! This is a very similar scenario to toddler potty training.

We would never stand by in silence when our toddlers or puppies manage successfully to hit the right spot. The level of enthusiasm that we have in this particular situation we also need to bestow on ourselves when we have successfully completed the routine part of any new habit we are sculpting in our brain.

There are a number of additional strategies that I have stumbled upon with experience that we could potentially use when creating habits.

Creating a new habit is like any skill and pardon the repetition, but we have to practice, practice, practice. Practice makes permanent. We also have to fail, reflect, revise and keep on going and sprinkle our attempts with a hefty dose of self-compassion, loving-kindness and minimal judgement in order to succeed.

We cannot learn without failing.

1. Why? Your Ikigai! We have got to know our WHY. The reason we want to make this change. For what purpose? Lose weight? Why? To get healthy? Why? Meditate. Why? Exercise? Why? And it's almost always a bigger why than you think. Writing your Ikigai (Ik-ee-guy) and 'whys' down and reading them daily gives us the inspiration to keep ongoing. Read more on your Ikigai later on.

2.'SETTLING OUR HEAD' Pardon me, you may never have heard this expression before or perhaps you have because you have a Northern Irish friend. This is a colloquial saying in Northern Ireland and roughly translated means 'clearing your headspace' or obtaining peace of mind.

If you cast your memory back to my explanation of the 'Upstairs/Downstairs model of the brain and the different characters within, it will become very clear to you why you need to 'settle our head'. If we want to make any 'change' in our lives which the emotional limbic brain will no doubt interpret as a threat to our survival (no matter how small and insignificant), we need the emotional brain to collaborate with our thinking brain. We can only do this if we market the new changes by taking 'tiny steps'. Believe me; it takes a lot more than reading any book or article on health and wellness, even if it does give us a huge dose of inspiration and enthusiasm. These emotions and feelings quickly haemorrhage. The best strategy is to target the characters in our heads and persuade them to behave, co-operate and get along by working in tandem. We 'Settle our heads' so that we can adopt the right mindset.

Let me introduce you to Professor BJ Foggs work. I believe Professor Fogg's method of tiny habits is a great negotiating tool to encourage collaboration between the upstairs and downstairs parts of our brain. Every habit has a Habit Loop; Cue - Routine- Reward and when the habit is repeated enough, the reward sets up a craving for the habit so that the habit gets repeated. We want to keep Ole Captain Basal Ganglia happy at all times.

There is one vital stage that gets overlooked by many, and it comes before the 'cue' step of the loop....it's the GETTING STARTED bit... We can all be full of good intentions, but it is the GETTING STARTED that proves one of the most difficult parts of introducing a habit. Going from doing absolutely nothing to doing something is very labour intensive, very! Professor BJ Fogg overcomes the frustration of this inertia by breaking down any new habit into a tiny habit, in fact, a ridiculously teeny, tiny habit. He suggests that if you want to create a new habit, you must first simplify the behaviour.

Make it ridiculously easy and fast to do.

Professor Fogg gives an example from his own life; flossing his teeth. After many frustrating years of failing to adopt this habit, he came up with the ingenious idea of flossing just one tooth after he brushed his teeth at night. That was the criteria for his success, successfully flossing one tooth. He had lowered his benchmark so low that it was impossible to fail. Even his downstairs brain, the emotional crew could cope with what appeared to be this insignificant change; one tooth. Every time he successfully flossed a tooth, a little dose of dopamine was released keeping 'Ole Captain Basal Ganglia' more than happy to code it as a habit. Once the habit of flossing one tooth was firmly embedded, it was almost effortless to floss his other teeth.

You might think that this is not enough. To make changes in my life, I use the 'Tiny Habit method' where appropriate. Let me tell you the story of learning to play the piano.

When I started piano lessons 18 months ago, my tiny habit was to practice ONE minute after school drop off each morning. Every morning, after I came through the front door after dropping the boys off to school and putting my bags down, I committed to sitting down at the piano and playing for ONE minute. Ridiculously simple! It was too easy not to do it. What I found is that after sitting down, I would play for at least 10 minutes, but the beauty of it was that I had lowered the bar so far that I felt great after a minute. Success to me was only ever ONE minute away. Imagine if I had started with the goal of practising TWENTY minutes two to three times a week. I can imagine my downstairs brain would have gone into lockdown mode after a week or so. If you make the new behaviour painful, a nuisance, an obligation or in any way negative, then a habit won't form because you won't be able to sustain it. Our downstairs brain is wired to avoid anything negative, so we need to shrink the habit, so it is ridiculously easy to achieve. We want our emotional and thinking brains singing from the same music sheet.

3. The Habit Loop - Test if for yourself.

It's really useful to understand the neuroscience behind habit formation and the habit loop. We need to plaster Cue - Routine- Reward on the front door and walls of our brains!

Test the neuroscience out for yourself. Become a habit detective and researcher in your own life.

Pick an existing habit or a habit you feel fairly confident you can do and dissect the Loop - Cue - Routine- Reward. Be curious. In the beginning, we also need a few quick wins to regain our confidence.

Just follow the three magic steps of the Loop ~ Cue - Routine - Reward and make your first habit teeny, tiny so that it's super achievable. This is your stepping stone for creating bigger habits in the future. You are looking to create a domino effect with your habits - and so there is magnificent power in starting TINY.

4. Be aware of the Stages of Habit Formation; forewarned is forearmed.

Habit Stages

I believe there are five distinct stages that most mortals go through in order to develop a habit. Think back to times when you were developing a habit whether you were successful or not. You might recognise these stages as I briefly describe them.

First Stage – High Energy: We have made the decision to incorporate the new habit into our life. We are full of energy, inspiration, enthusiasm, motivation, and we tell all your friends about it. To be honest, we tell everyone we meet, friend, or not because we are so excited. This time we are going to crack this new habit. We have almost convinced ourselves that we are already doing it and that it's going to be easy. There might even be a little bit of 'genius syndrome' floating in the air. We wonder why we had never thought of doing it before. The habit seems to be already integrated into our life, and we haven't even practised it. We are so fired up; we think it's impossible to fail. We manage our new habit for a few days and then, out of nowhere, our energy, inspiration, enthusiasm, and motivation dissipate. It is as if someone has turned off 'the switch', pulled the plug. However, we manage to continue on to...

Second Stage – Discomfort: We are going through a period of discomfort. It's almost physical but not quite. It's an irritation. We question whether or not it was a good idea to embark on the habit at all, how and when did we ever talk ourselves into even thinking we could do it? Why did we tell all our friends? Who were we fooling? Whose idea was it to even start? We want to run kicking and screaming from this habit that we have inflicted upon ourselves. Most people give up at this stage, and that's completely understandable, but this stage is really vital and very necessary. We falsely think we must be doing something wrong. In fact, we could not be further from the truth. Our brain chemistry is literally changing, and it's uncomfortable and really annoying. But we persevere, and we reach the next stage…

Third Stage – Comfort: we finally see the light at the end of the tunnel. The habit is becoming more familiar, and it's not uncomfortable to keep doing it. We have made your way through the 'neurochemistry storm', and things are settling down in our brain again. And finally, we reach...

Fourth Stage – Need: We actually need to do the habit because if we don't, we think something is missing in our life. The habit is automatic, and through our efforts, Ole Captain Basal Ganglia has pushed the 'autopilot button'. The new habit has been installed.

But we are not out of the wilderness...

Fifth Stage - Boredom/Complacency: There is a stage that sometimes creeps up on us unawares. Knowing that this stage might rear its ugly head might be just enough to prevent it from happening in the first place. This is the stage of boredom and complacency. Familiarity breeds contempt.

As much as the brain is lazy and loves working in habit/autopilot mode at times, it will struggle with boredom. The lure of the 'shiny new pleasure' aided by Party Animal Nucleus Accumbens will appear very attractive.

To counteract this; we need to add a little novelty to our habits without compromising the integrity of the habit loop. This could be a seasonal change, a new walking/running route, something small almost insignificant that makes a difference.

Reflection in your journal when things are going pear-shaped, alongside a healthy dose of self- compassion and loving-kindness are great tools for getting us back on track or, in this case, back in the loop. Life is full of curveballs in all shapes, sizes and coming possibly from multiple directions.

P.S. When Things Have Gone Pear-Shaped Strategy. When things go pear-shaped for me I use the rule of '3'.

If my regular routines are disrupted by holidays and illness and my cues, disappear then I rescue and reassure myself that it will take three days to get back into the swing of things.

For major obstacles, I give myself the wiggle room of three weeks.

And if I am looking for a change in my life and I introduce a new habit to my existing routine, I also use the Rule of '3':

3 days …… I will feel different

3 weeks….. I will notice the difference

3 months….Others will notice the difference

P.P.S. The Focus Fifteen Strategy. When I get stuck during my days, I put a timer on for fifteen minutes. That's the time I allocate to the task; I need to get started and overcome that 'I can't be bothered to do this' feeling. This strategy isn't necessarily for habits; it's for all the other mindless tasks we have to do that although add value to our lives also suck the life force from us, i.e. the ironing, the washing etc. etc.

If I'm still stuck … I let myself off the hook and realise that this 'stuckness' will pass; it will all get done at some time. Like, everyone, I'm imperfect and very human.

5. Exploit the power of the 'Personal Challenge' to create a personal law or code.

Many of the 'change gurus' also talk about the power of the epiphany and its miraculous ability to create changes in our life and at super speed but they readily dismiss this as a strategy because 'epiphanies' are not an everyday occurrence.

Think of the person that has just suffered a heart attack or any near-death experience. Almost immediately after such an event, their lifestyle totally changes, albeit we would never want to experience this extreme just to create positive change.

It might sound bizarre but I disagree with the gurus I think under special circumstances we can 'create an epiphany' - we need lots of grit and determination and bucket loads of willpower.

We decide to make one big change in our life for a specific period of time, possibly seven days, fourteen days, maybe even a month. We set this up as a personal challenge and commit to following it wholeheartedly 100%. After the time period has elapsed or somewhere in the middle of the challenge, we realise we are achieving amazing results. As a result, we could never go back to the way we were before.

We have literally created our own epiphany. We realise we cannot live without the habits we have adopted at breakneck speed. We would never have arrived at this conclusion without the personal challenge experiment. The only limitation of this approach is that it suffers from the novelty factor. We can only focus on a single major change at a time and capitalise on the successes without delay when we experience them.

NOTE: There are limits to the number of times that you can use the power of the 'Personal Challenge' because it takes up a lot of cerebral energy. We are relying heavily on willpower and overriding the 'feelings' of our emotional brain. If you do not plan fully for the 'Personal Challenge' approach… failure is inevitable.

Ironically the personal challenge may sound very like the 'Bridget Jones Approach' that we dismissed at the beginning of the book and again at the beginning of this chapter. There is a subtle difference in this scenario. With the personal challenge we have planned every detail, we have a more positive attitude, and we are not suffering from a 'knee jerk reaction' at a time when our lives have hit a low point. We are limiting it to one change at a time, not multiple changes.

The power of positive results gained during or after a personal challenge can quite literally shock us, and in so doing creates the epiphany, and if we are on the ball, we can quite literally change our habits overnight. We without realising it have reverse engineered the habit loop - REWARD - ROUTINE - CUE. Ole captain Basal Ganglia has been drenched in dopamine and has got the message. We want these new behaviours to become habits, and we want it immediately. We have been awarded the star pupil at the 'School of Habits', and our 'Habits' have been super glued into our brains and days.

6. Learning to use our superpower – our WILLPOWER efficiently. Any change we want to make in our life relies heavily on willpower but only initially until we have the new habit firmly programmed into our Basal Ganglia. In simple terms our willpower is motivating us to go; I WILL, I WILL, I WILL instead of the negative thoughts of our emotional brain - I WON'T, I WON'T, I WON'T!!

Willpower is ever vigilant and is alert for the cues you have devised for the beginning of your habit loop. Willpower also gives us that oomph! To follow through with the routine part of the habit loop. Eventually, the behaviour will be a habit and willpower is no longer necessary.

Your objective is to preserve the battery life of your Willpower at all costs. These are the three things that really drain your willpower:-

- Lack of sleep
- Too many decisions
- An over-sensitive emotional system.

Lack of sleep and our willpower is snookered. Willpower originates in our Prefrontal cortex Mr PFC- that's our thinking brain. It uses the same energy source that is used for making decisions, focus, putting things into perspective, pacifying Sergeant Major Amygdala and paying attention - all our higher executive functions.

It would shock you how many decisions we make on a daily basis. Even more shocking is the fact that many of those daily decisions are trivial, and we have been repeating the same trivial decisions almost every day of our life so far. There is a phenomenon known as 'decision fatigue'.

Did you ever wonder why we can make our best decisions first thing in the morning? We are more likely to enjoy a healthier breakfast and a good enough lunch, but our food choices rapidly go downhill at dinnertime, and as the night wears on 'junk food' seems much more appetising.

Decision fatigue has set in, and we're vulnerable. Using the 'Decide in Advance' tactic is very valuable. Deciding what you are wearing the next day, what you are eating the day before, how much you are going to drink at parties etc. - deciding in advance reduces the number of daily decisions we have to make.

Another one of my daily habits is to declutter both physically and mentally for fifteen minutes. Clutter comes at a price. It sabotages Mr PFC's attention and in so doing drains our willpower.

I want to make every effort to preserve my Willpower. If we are to make sure every day counts, we all need to preserve, maintain and increase our willpower and our daily habits need to support this.

Dealing with an overwrought emotional system which completely switches of Mr PFC's power source by pausing, breathing, meditating, having a gratitude and journaling practice are all fantastic activities to soothe the emotional brain. These activities act as a type of currency in a similar fashion to the banking system; we have to put in a lot of deposits before we can get a return and see the benefits. Moreover, we need to be careful. If there are no deposits and lots of withdrawals such as stress we can get into emotional debt very quickly. We are continually looking for ways to keep the downstairs characters happy.

7. Motivation

So, where does Motivation come in? I love science, and I love equations, and I would be doing you such a disservice if I did not introduce you to 'THE MOTIVATION EQUATION'.

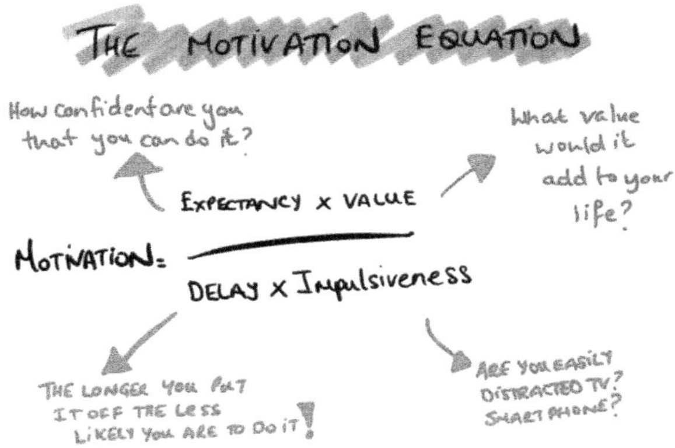

'Motivation is what gets you started. Habit is what keeps you going.' – Jim Ryan

I was first introduced to the Motivation Equation by Brian Johnson from the daily dose of inspiration from www.Optimise.me. This comes to me via my inbox every morning, and I have subscribed to this for over two years. It's definitely worthwhile joining his email list. I have learned more from Brian Johnson and The Twins than any degree, diploma or certificate I have completed.

The MOTIVATION EQUATION was formulated by Piers Steel, professor at the University of Calgary and is among the world's foremost researchers and speakers on the science of motivation and procrastination.

Motivation increases when you are confident that you can instil a new habit into your daily life, and motivation decreases when you delay getting started, AND you have lots of distractions in your life. Motivation really increases when you think the habits you are creating are really worthwhile and life-enhancing.

Perhaps you are trying to introduce too many habits all at once. We have all suffered from this syndrome. "Let's do it all at the same time" and so the more you ‘delay' in getting started, the greater the impact on your motivation levels.

Motivation goes up when you increase the top line and decrease your bottom line; simple maths!

And when motivation is running, kicking and screaming down the road, remember that we don't always have to feel motivated to do something.

We often think that we have to feel like doing something before we take action. On the contrary, often we need to take action and then if, by magic, the feeling will follow. In this case, motivation follows the action.

8. Think Throughs.... Planning for Failure.

It's inevitable. We can only learn through failure. And that is easier said than done.

I came across this concept in Gabrielle Oettinger's book "Rethinking Positive Thinking'. She advises that for every dream, or wish we want to make in our life; we need to plan for failure to increase our chances of success. It may sound counter-intuitive to plan for a failure but being overly optimistic can all too often jeopardise our chances of success.

We need to, therefore, think of the situations or obstacles that are going to get in our way, and we need to create IF/THEN strategies. For example: If such and such happens, I will do the following...and write them down, so it is not wishful thinking.

The upside of this strategy is that when things do go wrong, which inevitably they will, we are not relying on Mr PFC to rescue us. We have already cleverly decided in advance. Without If/Then plans we are sabotaged by our emotional downstairs crew, and they love to add fuel to the fire.

Michael Phelps and his coach worked with if/then strategies in the run-up to the Beijing Olympics in 2008. They endlessly practised situations that could go wrong in the pool. During his final race, his swimming goggles filled up with water as he entered the pool. This very situation had been imagined, and therefore did not have a detrimental effect on his performance; he went on to win his 8th gold medal. Without rehearsing these potential disasters, his performance may have been compromised.

9. Limiting beliefs about our abilities; for some of us, we feel like we have travelled around the vicious cycle of failure too many times, and we lack the ability to make changes. Here lies the problem. We need a 'mindset shift'. Our attitude to failure is crippling our efforts, not the failure itself. We use our failures as an opportunity to berate and shame ourselves once again - I'm useless/I'm a failure/I'm just not good at this/I've no willpower. Our failures are giving us vital clues not to try harder but paradoxically to try less. Our efforts may have pushed us into an emotional spin where the downstairs characters have totally taken over, and we are not making progress.

Taking time to reflect on our failures gives the downstairs characters airtime. We need to be curious about the failure or failures; what went wrong? Are there any patterns? Were our expectations just far too high? Were we trying to make far too many changes all at the same time?

Were we concentrating on one area of our health and wellbeing and neglecting all others at our peril? How many hours sleep did we get? Were we taking time to rest? Get comfortable with our failures and learn the lessons that they are trying to teach us. We cannot learn without failure.

I feel a little odd writing those last couple of paragraphs. I am no expert on learning the lessons from failure, so those paragraphs are written as a special reminder to me. It's only now that I'm starting to make friends with failure. At school, I thought you had to know the answers before the teachers actually starting teaching the topic. I still remember getting my first sum wrong. I can even remember where I was sitting in the classroom. I hated making mistakes. I thought it was some type of character defect. I can honestly say that the only area of my life that I don't care about making mistakes is when I'm cooking, even if I am entertaining a large crowd. For some unknown reason, I have this attitude that if things go wrong and I make mistakes, then I can learn from them and things can only get better. I am now borrowing this attitude for other areas of my life. As always, I am a work in progress.

Carol Dweck PhD is a Professor of Psychology at Stanford University, and she wrote a brilliant book 'The Power Of Mindset'. She describes two mind sets; a Growth Mind-set and a Fixed Mind-set. A Growth mindset creates a passion for learning, embraces challenges and setbacks and welcomes mistakes as an opportunity to learn. In contrast, a Fixed Mindset is embarrassed by its mistakes. It prioritises approval before learning. Interestingly I do love learning, but in lots of areas of my life, I realise I have a very rigid fixed mindset if I am asked to do something out of my comfort zone. Yes, it's that fear of looking stupid rearing its ugly head again just as it did when I got my first sum wrong.

Now I am making an effort not to hide my mistakes. Instead of trying to save face, I am learning to own up to my mistakes to myself and learn from them. The image of effortless perfection is exhausting. The boys are, thankfully, being taught this concept at school, so I am learning with them. They have taught me the power of the word 'yet'. If I am struggling with a task or am trying to create a new habit and things don't go to plan, instead of shaming myself I remind myself as they have role modelled to me to think that I haven't mastered it YET!

Needless to say, there are possibly a few mistakes throughout this book; I am cultivating a Growth Mindset in front of your very eyes.

10. Create a Habit Tracker and update it regularly. Create a chain: Don't break the chain.

This strategy is very simple but extremely effective.

At the end of each 'routine step' of the habit loop and after we rewarded ourselves with an appropriate 'goofy reward' we need to put a red cross on a habit tracker. As the days pass, we will have logged our successes as a chain of red crosses. As time goes by, we are inspired to keep up the momentum of completing the routine because we do not want to miss out on the addition of a red cross. Every time we reflect on the chain, serotonin is released, and we get a huge dose of satisfaction. We are proud of ourselves and rightly so. We get to the stage that we don't want to BREAK THE CHAIN. It is easier to do the habit than not to do it!

Piano experience. After practising for one minute, I would always reward myself by filling in a habit tracker I had created. I got this idea from the comedian Jerry Seinfield, and many others have referred to his practice of not breaking the chain.

Jerry Seinfield is one of the most successful comedians of all time. One of the secrets of his many successes is that he writes a new joke every day and then he marks it off on a calendar with a big red cross. After a few days, he has a chain of red crosses, and as the days pass by, the chain inevitably grows longer. His goal is not to break the chain. He doesn't focus on the results. He focuses on the process so that he is continually reinforcing his habit of writing a new joke every day. Many of these jokes never get used in his material, but that's not the goal. The goal is not to break the chain. And every time he places a red cross on the calendar, dopamine is released. Dopamine makes us feel good.

Feeling good makes us repeat the sequence, and as the chain grows longer, we get a little wave of satisfaction as serotonin - our happy hormone is released, and we get that glowing feeling of satisfaction.

Recently I have added to my habit tracker by writing my Ikigai and list of associated WHYs so I can see them when I'm ticking off the tracker. I get a chance to re-read my whys to reflect and reinforce why I am sticking to my habits in the first place. Memory is over-rated, so we need continual reminders as to the reason why we are putting in such an effort, and it gives us another dose of inspiration. So we keep doing what we are doing!

XXXXXXXXXXXXXXXXXXXXXXXXXXXXXXXXXXXXXXXX
XXXXXXXXXXXXXXXXXXXXXXXXXXXXXXXX

Carpe Diem ET Quotidie Postmodun - Seize the Day and Every Day Thereafter!

Wouldn't we all love to get out of bed and 'Carpe Diem' - Seize the Day'? That's the type of mojo most of us would love to dial into our days. Is it even possible? Modern life is messy and hectic. We need more than our 'To-Do' and 'Should Do' lists, our obligations and responsibilities or even our well-intentioned goals to propel us out of bed so that we can fully embrace everything our day and our lives have in store for us. There seems to be very little room for seizing the day these days; it feels very much like surviving the day is about the best we can manage. Truthfully we need to find our purpose; our WHY!

When I look back on my life, for most of it, I have only fleetingly thought of my 'Why' I have glossed over it. I have never spent any real-time figuring it out or writing it down. I have meandered along, ticking off life's milestones, dealing with the dramas when they arose and generally living my days' some great, some not so great. That's probably normal. From time to time, I would set some goals, achieve some, fail at some, create some new goals and carry on. I'd try different projects, complete some and disregard the rest that bored me or got the better of me.

The Japanese have a lovely concept for finding purpose in their lives. Ikigai (ik-ee-guy), it's an old Japanese teaching that's been thought to be responsible for the nation's long life expectancy. Ikigai is about finding joy in life through purpose. In other words, your Ikigai is what gets you out of bed every morning and keeps you going. Your Ikigai gives you direction, a reason for being, your raison d 'être.

I am fascinated by the work of Dan Buettner. In 2005, he wrote a cover story for the National Geographic on the secrets of longevity centred around the 'Blue Zones'. A Blue Zone is a region where people are statistically healthier and live longer than anywhere else in the world. There are currently five identified on earth; Sardinia in Italy; Loma Linda in California; Nicoya Peninsula in Costa Rica, Icaria in Greece; and the Okinawa Islands in Japan. When Dan travelled to these various regions, he noticed that each region had its own version of 'Ikigai'.

From his research, he is even more convinced that you have to be clear in your mind what your sense of purpose is and what you need to be able to summarise it in one sentence. His 'Ikigai' is going into cultures and distilling the lessons that the rest of us can learn from.

Everyone's Ikigai is different.

For me, it took me a while to find my 'Ikigai'. Like anything worth doing, you have to commit time to figure it out.

My one sentence 'Ikigai' is ....

'Add value to my life, my family and everyone else that I come in contact with, through my learning and experience.'

In fact, I have a 'one-word' Ikigai - 'Value'. To me, it means everything, and it's where I get my mojo. The word 'value' actually gives me a visceral tug that cannot be ignored.

That's my reason for getting out of bed in the morning. When I finally figured out my Ikigai; it was as if a lightbulb had just been switched on. It helps me focus on my daily habits and making my days really count. By doing these habits, I add tremendous value to my own life. In every way, I am in a much better place to add value to my family's life and everyone else around me. Making sure I get enough sleep, that I eat well, making sure I exercise, that I rest daily no longer seem a chore. I am continually linking the benefits of how I feel with my daily habits to my Ikigai, and my Ikigai keeps motivating me to follow through with them in the first place.

How can you find your Ikigai?

Finding your reason for being in life may seem easier said than done, but Dan offers some suggestions.

"Sit down with a piece of paper and make three columns, write 'what I love to do'. The second column should read 'what I'm good at,' and the third column should say 'what allows me to live my values'. Make a long list for each of those. Your Ikigai is the crossover section between all three, and you want to make sure you have an outlet for that in your life.'

I took another route to find my Ikigai. I took a bird's eye view of my current life; what my responsibilities were, what my obligations were, then I looked back on what I had achieved so far, what I enjoyed doing, what I was proud off, what I gravitated towards before I had responsibilities. I thought what I would do if all my financial responsibilities and all my other responsibilities were miraculously taken care off. I thought of the milestones I had hit in my life and then thought of the biggies that I'm about to hit. Those that mysteriously after you hit, make you feel almost invisible in today's world, you find yourself inside a vacuum; just at a time when you have a lot to give back to the world. How would I then spend my days? Certainly not by being invisible. I thought about how I wanted to be remembered by my family and friends, what legacy did I want to leave. I looked at my values; what was important to me, and with all of this, I looked for a consistent theme, joined the dots and came up my Irish version of an Ikigai.

Nobody ever jumps out of bed for goals alone, but if you wrap your goals up with your Ikigai, giving them an intrinsic quality, you will achieve great results surpassing all your expectations.

Having your own Ikigai completely shifts your mindset and gives you clarity and direction in your life. It gives you a darn good reason to 'seize the day'.

Do you manage to seize the day - Carpe Diem?

Do you survive the day - Superesse Dies?

Have you found your Ikigai? If not, spend time searching for it.

I am on a mission to seize my days and every day thereafter.

(Carpe Diem et Quotidie Postmodun).

What about you?

In the following chapters, I share the stories of my successes and strengths, shortcomings and failures and the lessons I've learned trying to live with my Ikigai. Each chapter gives rise to one or more micro habits that I have incorporated into my day to make them count. I hope the stories add value to you and your days so that together we can Carpe Diem et Quotidie Postmodun...

Seize the day and every day thereafter.

Sleep

I really get the importance of sleep. I preach it to my children and my clients.

However, since having children, it has been my Achilles heel.

Sleep was a real sticking point for me, and I felt ashamed of this. 'Do as I say not as I do'. Making sure Every Day Counts has saved my sanity and asking someone else for a little help worked.

This is how my evening used to play out. An evening would begin (and still does now) when I pick the boys up from school. By the time we're home, it's almost 5pm.

There's homework to be done, dinner to be eaten, kit bags to be unpacked, piano practice for one boy, guitar practice for the other, LAMDA practice for both, showers, reading covered and downtime to be inserted in there somewhere.

Bedtime was 8ish and lights out 8.30ish.

There were a lot of 'ishes'.

Funny after the boys began to sleep through the night and became more independent (i.e. taking their showers without supervision) I took my foot off the pedal as far as times were concerned. I became less rigid and a little more flexible, too flexible. I assumed the boys had been doing their bedtime routine for so long that we had this one covered.

Looking back, I was living with a false sense of security and paying the price. When they eventually slept, some nights after 9pm, I came downstairs to deal with the fall out of the evening - dishes to wash, repacking of kit bags, signing off on homework diaries. Throw in there a few distractions too such as phone notifications, unopened subscription emails to be read probably an article on how to get a 'Good Night's Sleep'. I would also try and squeeze in some 'biggie' on my over-packed 'to do' list so that I would feel I had accomplished something on that particular day. Finally, nail that feeling of validation. (Add to that the allure of my iPad - after all this was 'me time' supposedly). With no real bedtime or bedtime routine, I would finally give in and go up to bed. In bed, I had to look forward to catching up on the day's news, answering a few WhatsApp messages, challenging Judy, Isobel and Carol on the Words with Friends Apps and then Googling whatever took my fancy.

This I felt was my official 'me-time'. After all, I deserved it! I always felt a little virtuous because I had kicked the need to look at Facebook and the Daily Mail gossip section.

Ohh - did I mention hubby....he travelled a lot in the earlier part of the boys' childhood, so I just got used to doing my own thing - I didn't factor him into my evening routine at all - not good! Then I'd set my alarm on my Smartphone and off to sleep. Yes, I have brushed teeth and removed my make-up - well nearly all of it. Unofficial bedtime was anywhere between 10pm and 12.30pm.

I always had at the back of my mind in the earlier part of the day that I would be in bed at 10pm; more to the point I always fooled myself that my bedtime was actually 10pm - really? The reality was that I was far too busy, frantically 'catching up' on all the things I had put off earlier in the day to be in bed at

10pm. Irrespective of my bedtime I always got up at the same time 6.30am.

Yes, I was at the end of my tether - I hope that's not just an Irish saying. I was exasperated most nights going to bed and feeling full of resentment. We were definitely not having that Hollywood family type of evening that I'd seen in the movies, and I imagined I would be having with my children, (yes that was before I actually had children). I'd had enough. I needed to come up with a good enough 'why' to get to sleep on time.

Clearly, all the health-giving benefits of sleep were not getting through to ME.

Yet again, I was reminded that 'It's always easier to give advice than do it yourself '.

I value kindness, patience, consideration, and as I was tired most of the time, I was struggling to role model these values to my boys. This really bothered me. And then it hit me out of the blue - if I'm not striving to be the best version of myself - then how can I expect the boys to be the best versions of themselves? I needed to put on my own oxygen mask, get a grip on my sleep and end each day feeling a little more relaxed and satisfied. In the end, I went to a coach to help me in this area. I was ashamed I couldn't figure it out entirely for myself. Sometimes you need the help of someone else to shine a light on an area of your life that you are struggling with. We don't always have all the answers for ourselves. With her wonderful help, I was able to blast a limiting belief I had. This was it; I didn't deserve to rest or relax until everything was done.

Before children, I had always felt at the end of the day; I accomplished 'stuff'. It's hard to define 'stuff' - maybe because of your job, the people you interact with you got a certain amount of validation, and you feel you have done something worthwhile. As a mum, you get very little validation; your children are 'an infinity project'. You will never quite know if you are getting it right. You just have to know you are giving and doing your best. Blasting that limiting belief reframed my evening routine for me. I had to let myself off the hook.

As a Mum, I would never get everything done. My expectations were far too high, so I needed to figure out what were the most important things to get done. What actually added value to our family life.

Another insight was that when I went to bed by catching up on the news, emails, WhatsApp messages, playing 'Words with friends' - I was actually letting the rest of the world into my bedroom and sabotaging my 'me-time' which I had been so precious about. And I was never that type of girl anyway.

Lessons learned from my sleep' struggles'...

1. The time between picking up the boys and their bedtime is 'Supercharged'. I have to deal with their overwrought sensitive emotional limbic systems and make sense of their day for them. The thinking part of their brain - Prefrontal Cortex will not fully develop until they reach 25. They cannot make sense of lots of things that have happened to them during the day. And they have tried hard to be on their best behaviour during the day. They have had to follow all the 'school rules' that are making up for their 'immature prefrontal cortexes'. When they see me at the school gates, there is a

tsunami of emotion coming at me and not the sound of harps playing in the background that I had imagined at school pick up time, before I had children.

2. I don't faff anymore - I get kit bags packed, homework diaries checked off, and dishes are done BEFORE the boys go up the stairs. These tasks take twice as long to do after they are asleep. Boys can help too with them, and that's important.

3. The boys' bedtime routine is now sacrosanct once again. If they are not getting to bed on time, then I'm not getting to bed on time. They too are tired at the end of the day. There are going to be twin squabbles, teeth not brushed and other little things are forgotten about, so I need to be present, hovering in the periphery so this part of the evening goes as smoothly as possible. I have to remember that their 'Thinking Brains' have a long way to go until they are 25. Everything is emotional with them, and that's the place they are reacting from.

4. Lights out at 8.30pm for the boys.

5. 8.30pm is the start of my bedtime routine. I now create a 'buffer' between the end of the boys' day, and my' me time' and my bedtime. I need to recognise my 'downtime' and honour it. I have a bath or shower and change my clothes. I've done all I can do today. Tomorrow is another day.

6. 9pm - I have created a rule - no more iPhone, iPad, checking emails or any variation of the above. This rule saves me a lot of mental energy, and there's very little of that left at the end of the day. I have gotten over my FOMO (fear of missing out). I now realise I wasn't missing out at all.

7. 9pm to 10pm. I sit down with my husband without tapping on the iPhone or computer keys. We watch an episode of something on Netflix. We are more connected. The Netflix subscription is worth it for this alone.

8. I read a book rather than my Kindle for 15- 20 minutes, and I am now ready to sleep at 10.30pm. Just need to set the alarm clock.

9. I set the 'old fashioned' alarm clock that I bought years ago because I didn't want to use my iPhone alarm anymore. It took me a while, but I got there.

My 10th and last lesson is that striving to Make Every Day Count no longer starts in the morning when I get up as you might expect; it starts the night before at 8.30pm when the boys' lights go off.

Take it from me; sleep is the magic ingredient to making your days count.

Let me remind myself, and you what should happen during sleep....how had I forgotten?!

When our heads hit the pillow, and we fall asleep, our brains slip into some necessary 'offline processing'. There is some serious downstairs 'emotional system' tidying up to be done. We need this to ensure our brains are in tip-top condition for the next day. I imagine some of the characters:- Sergeant Major Amygdala, Madam Hypothalamus, Ole Captain Basal Ganglia and let's not forget Party Nucleus Accumbens and Mr PFC sitting down and switching on the Netflix version of our day, rerunning and feeling our experiences whether they were good or bad, matching them with previous experiences, making sense of our day. We're recovering from the day's emotional events and soothing the emotional system preparing it for the next day's adventures. It's a necessary recalibration of the emotional system.

This much-needed sleep restores the neural stairways between the emotional downstairs brain and the thinking upstairs brain. Our goal is to charge Mr PFC fully, so he is ready to meet the challenges of the new day. While other parts of the brain can function reasonably well when sleep-deprived, Mr PFC certainly cannot, and the downstairs characters are left running the show. Anything can happen!

So how about you?

How many hours do you sleep every night? Do you have a bedtime routine, or is it to fall into bed and hope for the best?

Have you noticed areas of your life affected by lack of sleep; irritability, lack of focus, poor food choices, especially for refined foods that promise a much-needed hit of energy?

What gets in your way of going to bed at a reasonable time? Write them down...

What is the first step you need to take to ensure you get enough sleep?

Apparently, sleep hours for true regenerative sleep are between 10pm, and 3 am.

Remember the expression 'every hour before midnight is worth two after midnight'? I thought my mother had made that up when she needed an excuse getting me to bed as a teenager. It turns out she was right.

Are you missing out on any precious hours of regenerative sleep?

Simplifying Your Life: Physical and Mental Decluttering

A-ha! The penny has finally dropped. My mother has been using the potent power of decluttering for decades. Alas, until now, I had never joined the dots.

She is a gritty, courageous lady. I imagine like most Mums. Some of the dramas she has had to deal with down through the years still cause the hairs on the back of neck to stand to attention when I think of them. She has always been - and still is - a rock to our family, her own family, her extended family and within the community. She can always be relied upon and has been there for me in some of my darkest moments, and I am very privileged to still get to talk to her almost daily on the phone and visit when I can.

In a little townland in Ireland, my Mum was using the magic strategy of 'decluttering' to sort out any situations when she felt overwhelmed decades before Marie Kondo and 'The Life-Changing Magic of Tidying Up' graced our bookshelves. Let me explain...

In we would rush from school; all five of us, and my mother would be tidying the 'messy drawer'. No one dared speak when the contents of the 'messy drawer' were laid bare on the kitchen table. We all knew that Mum was sorting out some problem in her head, and until that drawer was tidied, we were in a 'Do Not Disturb' zone. Once the drawer mentioned above was tidied, peace reigned, and Mum would have her superpowers back again. It was as if she had topped up her valuable mental energy, which gave her total clarity and peace of mind. Little did my Mum know that her ritual tidying of 'the messy drawer' was in effect switching off her 'emotional brain' and switching on her 'thinking brain' - she had stumbled across a very valuable neuroscience hack.

Decluttering is indeed a valuable neuroscience hack, and when you fully understand its benefits, you really reap the rewards from this activity.

Decluttering not only frees up physical space but mental space too and increases your mental energy; it also supercharges your willpower.

So how exactly does decluttering accomplish all of these beneficial side effects?

Just a quick recap of the functions of the Prefrontal cortex; it deals with rational thought, decision making and is home to your willpower. Left to its own devices without any interruption, it is happily 'thinking' of a bigger, brighter future for you. Well, that's how I've come to interpret it, but its Achilles heel is having to make too many decisions, this is when decision fatigue sets in.

Clutter in every area of my life increases the number of decisions I have to make almost on a daily basis, and my brain literally runs out of charge.

Willpower; fully depleted. Think about it: an overcrowded wardrobe leads to multiple decisions on what to wear in the morning. Too many skincare products, too many toiletries, too many household cleaning products, you can apply the 'too many' mantra to every aspect of the 'things' in your life.

It's at this point I hear my husband's voice echo in my head. He has spent years patiently (umm, perhaps not so patiently) reminding me that there should be a place for everything and everything in its place. For years I had conveniently chosen to ignore this bit of sage advice. After all, the husband is never a prophet in his own home.

Now I try to follow this little rule for most 'things' in my life, and I've had to eat humble pie because it works. Following this simple rule aids the decluttering process. Digital clutter is equally guilty of renting too much space in your head; too many subscriptions, emails bulging out of your inbox, Twitter, Facebook, WhatsApp, far too many notifications knocking at your cerebral door. Every piece of digital information leads to a myriad of decisions to be made; do I answer it now? Do I respond? Do I like it? Do I agree? Where do I file it? Should I buy it? Should I not buy it? This all leads to decision exhaustion.

I have probably been decluttering for a couple of years now and when I look back; the 'stuff' I had in my house fuelled my procrastination in many areas of my life. At times, I did not have enough mental energy to focus on the important decisions in my life. It was if I was stuck in my life because of the clutter I had gathered.

So where do you begin your decluttering mission? Get your hands on Marie Kondo's book, as mentioned earlier 'The Life-Changing Magic of Tidying Up'. Follow the nuggets of wisdom in this book and her life-changing method of decluttering your space. Mum's book - 'Tales of the Messy Drawer' has not made it to a bookshop near you (yet) but maybe you will see it out there one day.

Declutter for fifteen minutes daily. Quite simply, whatever area of your life that causes you most frustration, friction and therefore wears you down needs to be decluttered. Think about the times you walk around the house, and red flags pop in your head along the lines of I must sort that out/I should sort this out; whatever red flag is popping into your head the most, then this is the place to start. Anything that irritates you on a daily basis. Stop what you are doing and think - why does this annoy me so much? It's possible that you need to declutter any area connected with what you are doing.

Also, think of areas of your life that you are subtly marketed to continually. Marketing is very clever; its sole purpose is to push the buttons in your emotional brain. Think of products that claim to make you feel better, look better, products that make your life easier or promises to take years off of you. Yes, there are some products that do live up to their claims but not all, and some of those products are energy vampires, left unused on your shelves and renting valuable space in your head.

The other little mantra I try to adhere to is 'Do something each day that cannot be undone'.

Many of us spend much of our time doing things every day that have to be redone the next day. Hugely value-adding to your life but not validating. Decluttering and dealing immediately with the unloved treasure that you discarded cannot be undone. Here are some suggestions from my life, which were areas where once upon a time, I had to make too many decisions.

Personal

• What to wear? Your wardrobe and that includes sock drawer, underwear and shoes. Find the clothes you love to wear and ditch or donate the rest immediately without delay.

• Toiletries - unused, unloved products or beauty regimes that inflict too many steps into your morning and evening routine get rid of them. Keep it simple and find a brand you love and be loyal. It will save you money and mental energy in the long run.

• Reading Material - what books, magazines, newspapers need to go?

• Working space at home or in the office - What frustrates you most about this space? Jot it down and start to declutter.

Family

Your kitchen is the room in your house that you have to multi-task the most in. It has by far the most items in it; foods, utensils, books, cleaning items, appliances you use multiple times a day: your fridge, your freezer possibly your washing machine, your dryer. There are lots of opportunities to pack 'things' into this space. Think of all the kitchen gadgets that promised to make your life easier that you have bought but never quite got around to using. Spend time decluttering in this room, and you will not regret the results.

Decluttering your life will fuel success in all areas of your life. Who knew that your overflowing wardrobe, that overflowing sock drawer with socks that had lost their comrade, kitchen cupboards with just too many labour-saving gadgets could have such drastic effects on your much-needed willpower and prevent you forming habits that in the long run bring you happiness? I work on decluttering my life as a long term project. As my children hit various milestones, another round of decluttering arises, and when such areas are decluttered, it gives me the mental energy to deal with their next developmental stage.

For other times when I am overwhelmed by the mess, I have personally created making breakfast/lunch/dinner in my kitchen (yes I'm very messy). I try not to be messy, but if I am too organised during the cooking process, I become less creative....I know that's a big fat excuse, but I let myself off the hook by thinking that's my next habit to work on.

So, whenever I find myself in the situation of cleaning up the destruction I have created in the kitchen, I put the timer on for fifteen minutes (it is amazing what you can achieve in fifteen minutes) and I get to it.

I use this for post-dinner party massacres or other situations for example when I have two sets of cricket whites that have grass stains 'deeply engrained' all over them, and there's a cricket match tomorrow, and I just don't want to wash them, then I put on the 'magic fifteen-minute countdown' and I get moving.

PS. For nostalgic reasons, I still keep a messy drawer in my house for those times when the 'overwhelm' train is fast approaching, and I need a quick cure.

Thanks, Mum, for that wonderful habit.

Many of you will have enjoyed Marie Kondo's books and TV show which demonstrate the method of rolling clothing items. This means they are organised neatly in one layer and entirely visible to pluck out of the drawer whenever needed without causing mayhem. I really love to apply this to kitchen drawers with those pesky drying and dishcloths. Apart from the 'messy drawer'; all other drawers are now taken care of in my home.

Journaling; the Art of Mental Decluttering

I never leave home without my journal. Leonardo Da Vinci did the same. I'm in great company. My orange Dingbat A5 plus grid lined journals are my most prized possessions. Everything goes into them, and I mean everything. In fact, this book you are reading is a product of years of scribbled notes adapted from my thoughts, my 'A-ha' moments, my goals, my dreams, my wishes and my 'could do' list, my successes and failures and solutions to any problems that have crossed my path.

Anything that inspires me or makes me curious gets jotted down too.

Best of all, I jot down questions that I need answers to but need time to really think about. Once my question is scribbled down, I feel it settles my emotional system and switches on my thinking brain. Mr PFC is then truly engaged so that sometime later in the day or later in the week I get my answer. My worries are then not bouncing around the downstairs part of my brain, causing all types of havoc and upset. It's my Scarlett o' Hara approach to journaling and life... 'I will think about that tomorrow'. I hope you know of Scarlet O' Hara. Often the answer comes sooner than tomorrow when I am doing an unrelated repetitive, infinity job like washing the dishes, folding the clothes, putting out the rubbish – these are when the greatest insights come; creative incubation at its best. If I am looking for a solution to something that is really troubling me I write it down in block capitals, then I feel like I'm screaming out for an answer.

I have always favoured scribbling down my ideas and thoughts, and I use the landscape orientation of my journal basically I turn my journal around. Mostly I use a mind map approach and ask myself one simple question - What's on my mind? When I'm downloading everything from my mind onto paper, I just don't want it to be linear. Writing in horizontal lines reminds me of taking school exams. One exception to this is my Gratitude Practice and Blessings Practice that I have for my family and friends that have added value and add value to my life. I write more about that in a later chapter. I use my Lamy fountain pen to write these down. I feel it adds a little 'kudos' to my practices, and I write those in horizontal lines.

At Christmas, I bought both my boys and my husband their own Lamy fountain pens so that they are continually reminded of the importance of writing in this digital age. I have answered many of my most important questions not by 'Googling' them but by committing them to paper. I tell my boys that their fountain pens are a switch for their thinking brains, and it's as if they are personally knocking on Mr.PFC's door.

I am up at least a half an hour before everyone else in our house, and this is intentional. This is my sacred, golden time. I have more control over this part of my day than any other, and it's precious to me. My day starts the night before because I make sure I'm in bed early enough to protect my wake up time.

Once downstairs, I have a cuppa, sit at my kitchen table and commit everything in my head to paper. I have a Lamy fountain pen and a Bic multi-coloured clickable pen that are always within scribbling distance of my journal. I love colour in my life. A reminder to me that life is never just black and white.

When everything is out of my brain, I make sure I write down my Ikigai, my immediate and long term goals and then my could-do list...... I have renamed it my 'Could Do' list... because it feels like I have more control over it than a 'To Do' list. A 'To- Do' list feels like one long list of fat chores and painful obligations. Once I have written down my 'Could Do' list, I always ask myself two questions - What tasks if I completed today would add the most value to my life and my families? What task adds the least value to my life? Then I prioritise....

I always make a point of ticking off anything on my 'Could Do List...' that I have completed. I'm not missing out on those extra shots of dopamine and serotonin that will be released when those ticks are triumphantly annotated beside the completed task. As the week passes by, I flick through my journal to remind me of everything I have achieved, yet another chance for satisfying serotonin to be released.

My Habit Tracker lives at the back of my journal. Each night I check and make sure I have ticked off all the habits that I have completed during my day. For those habits that I have not managed to do, I make a note to focus on them during the next day. If the same habit comes up time and time again; I ask myself - What's not working for me with regards this habit? This then gives me an opportunity to reflect and revise my habit loop.

On the opposite page of my habit tracker I write out my one-word Ikigai VALUE in BIG BOLD COLOURED letters, and I create a mind map that branches out to form it - reminders of how completing my daily habits supports and honours my Ikigai.

Although I have a morning journal practice and a habit tracker practice at night; my journal is always with me so that I can always scribble down what's on my mind!

Over to you…

Clutter comes at a price, not just the price you pay at the checkout. It rents valuable space in your head. What areas of your life need to be decluttered?

Which area irritates you most? My advice is to start there – fifteen minutes at a time.

Lastly, what's on your mind?

Gratitude

I remember hearing "Be grateful for what you've got" once or twice when I was growing up, maybe a few more times.

My mother was right (and I can imagine the smile on her face when she realises I've actually written that down).

I'm not sure she was actually thinking of the serotonin-boosting effects of gratitude, the positive effect on my immune system or the benefits to my mental and physical health. My Mum was probably a little frustrated with one of us, and it was a very clever tactical way of getting out of any negotiation we were having with her at the time. We were probably teenagers. The teenage years of your life is that time of your life when you do actually want more of everything, and you want it NOW without the responsibility of paying for any of it or dealing with the consequences of it if it goes wrong. Nonetheless, she was right, and there is now oodles of scientific research to validate the positive benefits of gratitude and its ability to rewire your brain for the better.

We live in a world where we are continually sent messages that encourage us to focus on what we lack. Marketing really preys on our desires and fears. They have manipulated a very primal instinct in us; that survival instinct, to be accepted and belong to a tribe and it leaves us with that sinking feeling that we have not enough, or what we have is not good enough, OR we are not enough. We are actually quite good at doing this all by ourselves thank you very much. We all have our own 'yellow brick road adventure' to navigate just like Dorothy, the Scarecrow, Tinman and the cowardly Lion and all need a pair of 'shiny red shoes' to lead us home.

Being grateful and showing gratitude is like having a pair of Jimmy Choo's red shoes without the price tag.

Gratitude leads us back to self-acceptance, contentment, and that's home where we are at our best.

If you only create one habit from this book, then writing down three things you are grateful for every night is a great place to start.

Having a gratitude practice has been shown to increase your happiness by 25%.

Imagine if your income was boosted by 25%, your holiday entitlement was increased by 25% - you would be shouting from the rooftops! 25% is huge!!

Dare I say; I too had read repeatedly about gratitude and its benefits and still didn't manage to appreciate the effects. Then one day I did, and I did it again.....and I did it again, and I did it again, and quite soon I saw the benefits.

It's hard at first, and you might cheat in the beginning by being grateful for the same things over and over again, but then you start noticing the things in life to be grateful for and sometimes they are the little things and then you will be amazed at just what you notice to be grateful for. When you reach this stage, it's like someone has switched on a 'grateful switch'. When I read Rick Hanson's book - 'Hardwiring Happiness' it was the first time I truly understood why we are not automatically grateful for everything we have immediately without having to think and search for things to record, without in fact putting it into practice. We don't because our brains are wired with a negative bias. Our default is to look out for the bad things in life.

Our ancestors were brilliant at looking out for the negative. It was either to eat or be eaten for them. They survived and so we are here. We don't need to be that negative now to survive in modern times. If anything, we need to look for the positive, to be grateful.

On a side note, have you ever thought that if you are alive now, then those that went before you in your family came through The Stone Age, The Bronze Age, Iron Age, Middle Ages and so on? In recent times, our ancestors survived two World Wars, so there is no doubt they have made many, many sacrifices so that we could be here today. If I ever struggle with gratitude, I always come back to that.

Another bonus of having a gratitude practice is that you cannot be grateful and resentful at the same time. It's mentally impossible to hold a positive and negative emotion in your mind simultaneously. Immediately you start having a more positive outlook on life.

Having a gratitude practice can change your perception of yourself. We are forever critical, and I was too, sometimes I still am. We judge ourselves for ageing, our weight, our mistakes, the emotions we are having. This constant rejection of ourselves can deplete our self-worth. Gratitude slowly allows us to appreciate who we are, which leads us further down the yellow brick road, closer to self –acceptance and home.

Having a gratitude practice as a habit reduces the impact of challenges that you come across. You have increased your resilience because you are already looking for the good things in your life, especially the small things because these are the things we need the most when things go wrong.

Scientists have proved that being grateful increases serotonin in your brain. I used to think of serotonin exclusively as the happy hormone, but it does much more than that. Serotonin gives you that feeling of contentment and satisfaction, and it also buffers dopamine. That might sound strange that dopamine needs a buffer, but it does. We all love a bit of pleasure, but too much of a good thing can have an equal and opposite negative effect. Without serotonin, we would never know when we were satisfied when we've had enough.

Dopamine is a seeking hormone. That's why the internet is so addictive, you can seek the answer to just about any question that comes into your head, and that's why you go down so many rabbit holes when you are Googling something. You want hit after hit of dopamine, which might be great if you want to develop a new 'healthy habit', but not so good if you are looking for continual dopamine hits in other areas of your life that gives you pleasure; foods, chocolate, shopping, drugs…just about anything and these can all be marketed to you etc. We need a way to feel contented, satisfied, but we have to stop and think about it. It's not immediate.

A daily practice of gratitude will increase your serotonin levels and leave you contented and satisfied and not on that eternal search for more. We have enough, and by being grateful, we soon realise that we are enough.

So listen to your mother, put your Red Jimmy Choo's on and be grateful.

Thanks, Mum, I am very grateful for you.

Gratitude soothes the characters in the emotional downstairs part of your brain.

They are reassured that you know that you are doing just fine and are satisfied with your life. That's how I like to think about it.

Do you have a gratitude practice?

If not…start straight away, why wait? It will add real value to your life, and you will soon find more reasons to 'Make Every Day Count'.

Right now, write down three things you are grateful for.

Haven't we made eating complicated?

For thousands of years, humans have eaten well, stayed healthy, survived and managed to successfully pass on their genes without nutritional scientists, blogs, Instagram posts, Twitter feeds or even knowing what an antioxidant is.

Considering we are constantly bombarded with 'healthy eating' messages, I wonder where have we gone so badly wrong, with the 'Eat' bit of our days? This constant stream of healthy eating messages is very noble, but the messages are getting drowned out with the need to survive, not the need to thrive. As a species, we need to look good for the tribe in order to belong.

Some of these messages are also getting very confusing. These are the lessons that I have learned with the 'Eat' part of my day (pssst I am supposed to know what I am doing. I have a Diploma in Nutritional Therapy, worked with lots of lovely clients and had a great experience as the owner of a health shop). We all tend to use the wrong success criteria; be careful what you wish for, your wishes may not come true. I remember going on my first 'diet' when I was 26 - that's practically ancient by today's standards. Growing up, I never remember my mother being on a diet, NEVER. There was no association in our house between the food we ate and weight loss. I can't even remember weighing scales. I was definitely a size 12 at 25 and in today's fashion climate that is considered a 'plus-size model'. In 1995 I travelled and worked as a Pharmacist in Australia, and I blossomed out there, probably hit a size 16. I blamed the negative effect of crossing the equator and living upside down for a year. The reality is that I can pinpoint the cause of my weight gain - It was the carrot cake in a little cafe called 'Mickey's' in Paddington, Sydney. I hope it is still there. My cousin and I would walk there every night and order a piece each. We congratulated ourselves on the 'walking bit' by getting the cake. We even convinced ourselves that because it had the word 'carrot' in the description that we were on to a winner (it was 1995).

Even though I don't buy into the calories in/calories out theory of weight loss; we were never going to out-walk that slice of carrot cake because it was humongous. We would have needed to walk all over Sydney at least twice.

(Just as a side note; Mickey's carrot cake was and still is the best carrot cake I have ever tasted in my life, and I still say that almost 30 years later. Imagine if we had missed out on that experience?!)

I am nearly 5′5″ and have been a size 10, a size 12, size 14 and a size 16 as the story above illustrates. I have been happy and miserable in equal measures at all of these sizes. So I now have historical data on myself (N=1) that reaching that 'perceived perfect size' is not the root of all happiness. Apologies though, I have not managed to do any randomised, double-blind studies on the above observation.

As women, why are we SO concerned with our size? I know the answer is obvious: we want to look good. Who doesn't? But why do we have this burning need to go to such extremes to look good?

Our evolutionary wiring needed us to be attractive to ensure not only our survival but the survival of the human race. I'm sure Darwin has some theory that proves this 'need'. Our biological imperative is to be attractive; therefore, for many of us, this has fuelled the never-ending compulsion to diet in order to achieve the tribe's new ideal of desirability and acceptability. There is a need not to be judged.

Humans are social animals, and there is also an evolutionary need to belong to a tribe. The only problem is that the measure of 'attractiveness' keeps changing within the tribe; often within a decade. The result is that we are ruled by a 'number on a scale or 'a size' and now our bodies are confused as well as our brains.

What is weight anyway?

"The number on the scale can only give you a numerical reflection of your relationship with gravity. That's it. It cannot measure beauty, talent, purpose, life force, possibility, strength or love. Don't give the scale more power than it has earned". - Dr Steve Maraboli

In her book 'The Thin Woman's Brain', Dilia Suriel summarises the changes beautifully within the tribe with the passage of time. From the 1950s through the 1960s, the voluptuous full-figured shapes of Marilyn Monroe and Jane Mansfield were celebrated...the secret why my mother never went on a diet. In her time, she was the perfect size. There were very few glossy magazines for her to flick through or with five children she had limited or no time to look at them. There was no social media either to make her feel envious and guilty.

In the late 1960s, Twiggy came along and made skinny an 'inny'. Her trademarks were her blonde, pixie haircut and her size 8 slim, boyish body. Curves were out, and the diet industry exploded. In contrast, Marilyn Monroe's weight fluctuated between 118lbs and 140lbs and made her anywhere between size 10 and 14.

During the 1970s and 1980s, models gradually became taller, thinner and began to show toned muscle definition. Larger breasts made a fashion comeback.

The late 1990s brought in tall, very thin models with no visible body fat and muscles highly toned by working out. Large breasts remained in style but were very rare in this body type without the help of breast implants.

Models in the 1970s weighed 8% less than the average woman; by the 1990s models weighed 23% less. In 2017 the average woman weighed 11st and wore a dress size 16.

A survey conducted by Mintel uncovered that almost half (48%) of the British population have tried to lose weight in 2016. That figure rose to 57% when researchers just looked at the results for women. To add to this for those that were trying to lose weight, almost two thirds (64%) said they do so "all or most of the time."

It appears men are now under the same pressure and scrutiny to look good and that's without this evolutionary curse. It's now fuelled by a 21st-century need - gender equality at last.

So in summary, any conversations about the 'EAT' subject today slips very quickly into a conversation about weight and that everlasting burning question - what is the newest, best, quickest weight loss diet out there on the market to follow? What have you tried? What works? Eating to maintain your health and thrive comes a little further down the pecking scale.

Survival as always is our default setting. I think it's important to answer some burning questions at this stage, so you never have to waste a moment thinking about them. This will do wonders for your emotional limbic system; this will help you let go of any needless worry and finally let your Pre Frontal Cortex get on with its job of thinking and planning to help you create a great future without the deprivation of having to follow a diet... a future where you are not only surviving but thriving.

You are attractive no matter what size you are.... if you are reading this then you are a survivor, and you belong.

Your genes have been passed down successfully from generation to generation to generation to get to you. You're here! That's it, wonder no more! And, you have ALL the information you need to 'get into the best shape for you' not a shape dictated by the outside world and media.

In the 1990s, for me to look attractive, I would have had to be stretched almost 5 inches and shrink my 'plus size 12'. No matter how many squats I did or how many perfect meals I prepared, my thighs were never going to look like Elle Macpherson's, but my emotional limbic system thought they should and were necessary for my survival. Its sole purpose was to help me survive and be part of the tribe.

So, we are now ready to begin! If I sat you down with a pen and paper and got you to jot down the top 3 eating tips to keep the human species healthy and living well...... I bet you could do it.

You don't need another 'diet book'. Nobody is going to discover something new that will give you instant weight loss. There is no undiscovered 'superfood' or external product out there with a magical solution.

So our extrinsic motivators to 'look good' as society dictates to stop our 'girlfriends' judging us because we are judging them or our motivation to hit that perfect jean size or number on the weighing scales is not nearly enough to propel us to success and help us thrive. We need a different driver an intrinsic motivator. We need to switch from looking good to feeling good. Feeling good is measured by our energy levels and our moods, whether they are both high or low. And although these are very subjective, we can measure them on a daily basis. You have immediate feedback!

Going on a six-week diet, we fool ourselves into getting quick results and that six weeks is all it takes. In fact, we expect results. Often we sabotage our efforts by these unrealistic expectations. A farmer would never plant a seed and dig it up six weeks later to see what was happening. He would give the seed all the nourishment it needed and wait, and continue to nourish and wait and continue to nourish and wait, and then reap the rewards.

The Neuroscience of Yo-Yo dieting.

Previously I have tried numerous food philosophies (diets, really) which set me up for total and abysmal failure. I would read up on the latest nutrition research, buy the accompanying 'diet' book and go hell for leather. New recipes, new shopping lists, maybe a visit to a speciality shop to get those specially mentioned 'health-promoting ingredients' perhaps that had never even made it into my pantry before.

I have lost count of the number of coconut flour packets I have stealthily put in the food recycling bin.

Food became a scientific experiment and totally lost its pleasure. Breakfasts were new, lunches were new, dinners were all new, but I was determined time and time again and used every ounce of willpower. And believe me I am good at following protocols, but at the six-week point, my willpower vanished, and inspiration had gone up in a puff of smoke. This would happen on a cycle as regular as clockwork.

As someone that has studied nutrition, you might think it strange that I was following 'diets'. In the strictest sense, they were more like food philosophies, whether it was gluten-free, dairy-free, clean eating. It is always more frustrating because I am supposed to know what I am doing, but knowledge and learning can make us even tougher on ourselves. Add throw in a bit of what I call 'Perfection Paralysis' – you look at all the other perceived voices of authority on nutrition, and they have all these Instagram feeds of the wonderful colourful foods they are having, and you feel 'a failure' even though your diet is probably 'good enough' - it's at the stage that perfection has obliterated goodness.

I almost came to the conclusion it was another form of 'food craziness' – and on some level an eating disorder. There was also an after effect of my 'perfect eating' attempts, which is aptly called the counter-regulatory effect otherwise known as 'What the Hell' effect and you eat everything in sight. If you can't be perfect, then what's the point? Looking back, this is so destructive and akin to yo-yo dieting.

Since studying neuroscience and getting to know the workings of my brain, I now understand why I was continually setting myself up for failure. Every time I picked one of those clean eating regimes, it was just far too many changes, too quickly, and my emotional limbic system just went into 'limbic spin'. I imagine my prefrontal cortex picking a new food philosophy, completely oblivious to the 'feelings' of my limbic system and going it alone thinking that willpower would win the day.

From my experience, the prefrontal cortex, teeth-gritting, brain gritting willpower method runs out of steam at about the six weeks mark. Up until then, I was going great guns, but it took every ounce of willpower and then it vanished like a magician's assistant - in a puff of smoke!

Now, my approach to my nutrition and the 'Eat' part of my day is dialled way back, and it is so darn liberating. The 'Eat' part of my day needs to be consistent and not a series of six-week cycles followed by a fall from grace. I have looked at numerous food philosophies and diets; paleo, vegan, clean eating, low fat etc. and looked at what they have in common.

Two things they all agree on is:-

1.) Increase your vegetables

2.) Reduce refined carbohydrates (The Junk).

Nothing out there recommends a reduction in vegetables or an increase in refined carbohydrates, i.e. sugar, cakes, biscuits, cookies, muffins etc. so I have gone back to basics, and this is what I stick too.

I eat more vegetables, AND I cut out processed foods and refined carbohydrates. Monday to Friday, I keep it simple - real simple. I stick to a set of meals I have had for the longest time. Food I can cook without a recipe book. I call these my default recipes and I bet you have yours too. Over time I have managed to add a variety of vegetables to these meals, which adds the necessary variety which the brain craves. I have a few caveats because I am not perfect and as my Aunty Tilly always said' "We were never meant to be perfect here on Earth, if you were perfect you'd be already in Heaven". That sooooo takes the pressure off! Nature would never approach the "EAT' problem like we do. Nature always starts where it's at and makes incremental improvements over time. None of this 'throw everything out and start from scratch again'. Anything new that we introduce into our lives has to have a corresponding habit loop to go with it. You can't achieve one without the other, and it takes effort.

Genius syndrome - we all suffer from it. We imagine we can introduce something new to our lives without carefully scripting a habit. It has everything to do with neuroplasticity. You can teach an old dog new tricks, but you have to give it the right treats. Habits are the secret sauce to the 'Eat' part of our day and come to think of it every other part of our day too.

I am still 5'5", and I think about size 11, I am a Mum to 10-year-old twin boys, and I strive to be a good role model.

Some days I could win awards for my efforts. Other days don't go so well, but I want food just to be food and to be enjoyed as my mum taught me.

I want the boys to be able to differentiate between real food and fake food and to teach them about marketing and how to navigate through the shiny bright packages and health claims. Mostly I want them to eat their veg and ditch the rubbish and hand that down to their children and their children's children.

I want them to see me eat my colourful veg, especially 'green' and mirror what I do. I want to teach them the basics of cooking so they can create 'our family default meals' and replicate them in their own families.

I have a window of opportunity to do this, which is fading fast, so I am going to grasp it with both hands and waste less time finding 'the perfect diet'.

'If you fail to plan, you are planning to fail!' by Benjamin Franklin sums it up beautifully.

When the boys were younger, we would never leave home without having a clear plan of what we were going to feed them. Most times we had to bring it with us. We left nothing to chance.

Looking back, it was like military planning; otherwise chaos would descend, and we would have to deal with two very unhappy boys, and two very unhappy parents to boot! Adults are just grown-up children.

We have a window of sixteen hours every day where we can potentially think about food. Unless we plan what we are going to eat in a particular day we can be paralysed with lots of 'food-related' decisions - 'What am I going to eat today – for breakfast, for lunch, for dinner, when I am bored, when I am angry, when I am tired?

These questions can circulate in a continuous loop in our brains, wasting precious brain energy-depleting our precious willpower, revving up our emotional brain.

Remember, we are always thinking about survival. Bottom line is we need to plan most of our daily food in advance. If you haven't decided for yourself, there are a lot of companies out there making those decisions on your behalf and their sales marketing message play to your vulnerable, emotional limbic system. Think of the messages various advertisements of food send out – happy families, people having fun.....the big message being that if you are not eating their product, then you are missing out. We just cannot fly by the seat of our pants and make adequate food decisions all the time. People estimate that, on average, they make about fifteen food-related decisions each day. But the truth is, they make more than fifteen times that....more than two hundred such decisions. Poor Mr PFC has his work cut out for him. If there is no preplanning, he has to at times deal with an overwrought emotional limbic system which is caught up potentially somewhere in the HALT loop - Hungry, Angry, Lonely or Tired or a combination of them all. We need to decide in advance!

I manage to plan for the weekdays, three days at a time, and at the weekend I am a little more flexible. Default meals and making incremental improvements to these meals!!!

Use willpower wisely once when shopping not multiple times when you have bought the product, and it's lurking in your cupboard even if it's out of sight.

Controlling your environment, that is the contents of your kitchen cupboards, is the biggest contributor to your success. Online food shopping is so handy. Going food shopping to the supermarket is up there with going onto the battlefield.

Modern marketing is highly sophisticated. Yes, the supermarket is aptly named – 'super' good at marketing to you! Packaging, colours, smells are very cleverly created, so both your reward pathways and your emotional brain are continually stimulated and manipulated. The emotional brain is much faster to react and can hijack the thinking brain, so the thinking brain has no chance. I avoid it at all costs. My aim is to do 75% of my shop online and then pick up 'bits and pieces' during the week. My strategy is to reduce the number of decisions I have to make concerning food. You automatically switch off most of the clever marketing when you shop online because you really need to know what you are going to buy before you chose this method of shopping. Online shopping really stacks the odds in your favour by reducing your choices and your distractions. I also buy far less .You definitely have to decide in advance.... the only way to shop! Food is so emotional. Think back to when you were a baby. Ok, you can't actually think back that far, but you can imagine it.

As a baby, every time you were fed, you were held by someone. You were getting fed emotionally as well as physically. The cuddle hormone 'Oxytocin cursed through your body and it felt good. We felt safe. It's almost that with our food choices we want to return to that state with someone else taking responsibility for us. As adults, we can at times be caught in the trap of feeding our unmet emotional needs, using food not as a source of nutrition but as a 'mood fixer.' It's quick, convenient and easy to walk into the kitchen for your fix and food manufacturers are only too happy to help us.

Some foods have huge emotional significance. Quality Street has been super glued into my DNA. My Dad brought my mum an ounce of Quality Street every time he came to see her when they were courting. I have had access to the contents of a tin of Quality Street for every one of my forty-eight Christmas's that is until last Christmas. Christmas was not Christmas in my mind if I didn't tuck into a tin of Quality Street. Santa may have gone, but Quality Street would never let me down. (Mmmm...Have you noticed though that the tins have gotten smaller over the years? And Nestle has mucked around with the formulations. How dare they mess with my childhood memories!)

As number four of five children, way down in the pecking order I got to love 'the rejects' - the orange crème, the coffee crème, and the fudge one - sorry - maybe some of these are your favourites. Since setting up my own home, Quality Street was one of the first automatic festive purchases. One Christmas I realised that I was the only person eating all the Quality Street. My husband and children don't hold that emotional bond to them, so for years, I have ended up eating the rejects and the popular ones. Not a good place to be.

On that note I have other trigger foods...we all have them. The reward pathway associated with these foods is well worn. Interestingly dopamine is released even with the anticipation of these trigger foods. Identify your trigger foods because they have very well worn circuits in your brain. Very hard to resist. Don't buy them and yet again use that willpower wisely at the till. Sometimes though…I do need a chocolate fix, and it's not 85% organic and raw version. It's the bog-standard Dairy Milk chocolate found on every corner shop shelf I give in because it's a super quick way of soothing myself.

Sometimes life throws you curve balls. I am not so worried about this as long as I acknowledge my emotions, name them, tame them and move on. To counteract that energy zapping feeling of deprivation too...the emotional limbic system hates any sniff of deprivation or missing out I never say any foods are off-limits. It's a bit like the pink elephant phenomenon. If you are told not to think of a 'pink elephant' that's all you keep thinking off. The same effect happens for forbidden foods.

Eat foods that your great-grandmother would recognise. I love this concept because great-grandma could probably identify all the individual ingredients on her plate as nothing was processed. BUT my great-grandma had way fewer choices.

She had very few opportunities to be out and about, no cars, no long commute, and no planes. I am almost sure that eating on the street was 'not the 'done thing' in those days, and there was no such thing as 'fast food'. The food industry had not exploded. Food was more expensive, so more value was put on it. Food manufacturers were not so sophisticated that they employed 'food scientists' to figure out 'the bliss point' that totally lights up your 'Party Animal and the associated reward centres.

As mentioned before, these food products that light up the reward centre release almost pharmaceutical doses of dopamine and are very hard to resist even to the most virtuous of us out there. I want to introduce you to Michael Pollan and his simple food rules.

Now, if I had to send a special envoy to meet with Aliens that had taken over our planet and they needed human nutrition information to ensure our survival, I would without a doubt send Michael Pollan, the author of Food Rules - An Eaters Manual.

I have read well over 200 books, listened to countless podcasts, interviews on nutrition. But this book has had by far the greatest impact on me, purely because its message is very simple. It has brought me back down to earth! It reminded me that I ate food, real food most of the time.

His message is "EAT FOOD. NOT TOO MUCH. MOSTLY PLANTS." And the blurb on the back of his book summaries the contents of his book beautifully.

"Seven simple words of plain English. In Food Rules, internationally acclaimed journalist Michael Pollan gives us straightforward and invaluable rules from these seven words for day-to-day living, such as avoiding food advertised on TV or that your recent ancestors wouldn't recognise. These rules are simply designed to help you eat real food in reasonable amounts. Phrased in everyday language and collected from grandmothers, folk wisdom, science and common sense from around the world, this book is all you need to eat healthily, dine happily and live well."

In summary, the book contains 64 simple (and entertaining) rules to keep you out of trouble as far as food is concerned. These are my favourites...

1. Eat food, and that's real food, not fake food or food designed by food scientists.

2. Don't eat anything your great-grandmother wouldn't recognise as food – avoid food products containing ingredients that no ordinary human would keep in their kitchen.

3. Avoid foods that have some form of sugar listed among the top three ingredients.

4. Avoid foods that contain more than five ingredients.

5. Avoid food products containing ingredients a nine-year-old cannot pronounce.

6. Avoid food products that make health claims - these are often products of modern food science and companies with big marketing budgets.

7. Avoid foods that are advertised on TV.

8. Eat foods made from ingredients that you can picture in their raw state or growing in nature.

9. Eat only foods that have been cooked by humans.

10. Don't ingest foods made in places where everyone is required to wear a surgical cap.

11. If it came from a plant, eat it: if it was made in a plant, don't.

12. Eat mostly plants, especially leaves.

13. Eat your colours. This applies to vegetables.

14. Eat animals that have eaten well themselves.

15. The whiter the bread, the sooner you'll be dead.

16. Eat all the junk food you want as long as you cook it yourself.

17. Eat when you are hungry, not when you are bored.

18. Buy smaller glasses and plates.

19. Cook.

20. Break the rules once and a while.

And one of my own.....Food made with love with family and friends is always worth having.

So thank you, Mr Pollan, all credit goes to you for putting the 'common sense' back into food for me. Now it's time to put it into common practice. And my final lesson on the subject of 'EAT'. They say you can't exercise your way out of a bad diet. To this, I want to add a little more; that you can't eat your way out of stress.

I remember sitting my final exams on nutrition and devising elaborate nutrition strategies for my theoretical clients, strategies that in reality, no one could sustain.

Eat a rainbow coloured selection of vegetables daily, always include the colour green, eliminate processed foods and refined carbohydrates and adopt stress management techniques were always part of my answers. I remember thinking about the stress component and feeling a tad disheartened. We are humans, we live busy lives, and we are stressed. We need stress, we wouldn't have survived without it, but we also need ways of dealing with it in our fast-paced 21st-century life.

You may have a perfect diet: if you don't buffer the effects of stress in your life or attaining that 'perfect diet' is way too stressful for you, then you won't reap the benefits of it. Lighten up; your efforts are in vain.

Eat is only one part of the puzzle, Sleep, Eat, Move and Rest, our mindset and keeping things simple are all equally important. We need to address the basics in all areas of our life to build a solid foundation, so we not only survive in the tribe but thrive in the tribe.

Let me give you a little helping hand.

I. Eat three meals a day; Breakfast, Lunch and Dinner – nothing else.

II. Vegetables and Fruit (not fruit and vegetables); 50% of your plate needs to be vegetables. If the type of breakfast you are eating does not lend itself to vegetables, then eat fruit; mainly berries and apples and pears.

III. Promote your vegetables to the 'Main course'. They are long overdue a promotion from their 'side dish' supporting role.

Please do not underestimate the magical power of these Eat Habits.

I have studied and experimented with nutrition for almost twenty years, worked with lots of clients and advised many lovely customers in my health shop. I have read possibly too many nutrition books. Dare I say I have been up until now on a crusade to find that elusive 'perfect diet'. So I can confidently declare that I have tried all sorts of food philosophies.

I have enjoyed many of my nutrition adventures, but there have been times when I have wandered of the path of good nutrition and righteousness and been crippled with too much 'nutrition information' and self-criticism! Yes, as I mentioned before I was a martyr to the 'Eat Well' campaign, and for me, it was just not sustainable.

Actually, I had become a nutrition bore. In creating my EAT HABITS, I have been heavily influenced by two books in particular. 'Brightline Eating' by Susan Peirce Thompson and 'Eat to Live' by Joel Fuhrman. I read them at a time that they fitted into my own emerging food philosophy. Fast forward to today, and I feel totally liberated by the EAT HABITS that I follow. On any one particular week, I can follow a vegan, vegetarian, gluten-free, dairy-free, paleo, raw food, Mediterranean food philosophy. In truth, I am a 'sugarless food philosophy tart' but if I were to sum up my actual 'eating style' it would be this...predominantly plant-based with the added focus on colour, flavour and texture.

PS - I concentrate on getting vegetables into my diet and some fruit. Oddly enough, the protein, carbohydrates and fats take care of themselves. I am no longer obsessed with getting enough protein in my diet, or whether I'm low fat, high fat, low carb, high carb or any other combinations. When I focus on meeting my vegetable targets, for some reason, magically everything else seems to take care of itself without the head chatter. Try it for yourself and see.

In the last decade there have just been too many food rules that have popped up almost on a monthly basis adding to our mental noise; increase your veg, eat three meals a day, no more and the rest will take care of itself.

Consider this too: how many times have you set in place so many food restrictions that when you went out to eat, went on holidays etc. you couldn't keep up with your own food criteria? As far as I am aware and in my experience, vegetables are available all over the world and at any time of the year. Every restaurant menu, hotel buffet, chiller section in supermarkets have vegetables on offer. We just need to be a little creative and promote them to the 'dish of the day!'

Creating that gargantuan shift in my mind that vegetables are the stars of the show at lunch and dinner and totally deserved the lion's share of space on my plates. Now, no one is leaving 'my vegetables' in the corner of my (round) plate. This has been a real game-changer for me. Add to this the ritual of eating only three meals a day; Breakfast, Lunch and Dinner with no snacking in between has catapulted me into nutrition nirvana. Well almost!

Let me point you in the direction of 'nutrition nirvana' as I share the lessons I have learned along the way.

Lesson No .1 - Combining the two 'Eat Habits'

Making sure that half of your plate consists of vegetables, fruit (berries) at breakfast really satisfies the needs of the body. Our bodies and brains love consistency and really struggle with uncertainty. Our survival is their main priority; missed meals, sudden changes inundate the brain with alarm signals. Although eating meals at the same time each day is a great idea, eating the same meals every day can often lead to 'food apathy' and the search for that little bit extra on the side... this often leads to the big bit on the side. Promoting vegetables to the main dish and letting everything else become your side dish or accompaniment introduces a new level of flexibility to your mealtimes.

Just sit and think for a minute of all the varieties of vegetables we have access to.

Vegetables are such a versatile food group to cook with.... and so easy to flavour and literally spice up. A survey commissioned by Ocado in 2015 has revealed that, despite owning, on average, six recipe books, Britons are stuck in a nine-meal rut.

The survey contained 2000 adults, and they used the same nine dishes on rotation, rarely introducing new, exciting concoctions to their repertoires. So how do we create this shift, this switch.... where vegetables become your heroes?

Lesson No.2 - Setting the scene

Before you even get started, you have to prepare your environment, and in this case, that means your kitchen and especially your fridge. Your fridge will become your new best friend, often underused and overlooked. You have to get your fridge to work for you.

In the past, I have quickly opened the door, closed it within one breath because I didn't want to do battle with the contents that lay within. I want my fridge to look like one of those top dollar American dramas. You know that scene where they open the fridge, and it's brimming with colour, and you can almost smell the freshness leaping out of your TV. I'm not talking about the American sitcoms where the fridges are full of junk food, leftover pizza and cans of beer. That would have appealed to me as a student when there was actually nothing in my fridge because back then I was buying food with the longest expiry date with zero nutrition. Let's go for the fridge in the glossy American dramas.

Your fridge, you need to look at it daily, do a quick one-two check of what's in there, what needs to be used up etc. and once a week a more forensic inspection. All of us waste food to some degree, but sometimes there is a lag phase where it sits in our fridge waiting for a miracle to happen. We know it's there, but we don't want to deal with it. Fridge inspection the night before the bins are collected really works for me. While you are at it, have a look in your cupboards. Yes, the ones that holds your saucepans, your baking trays, your plastic containers etc.

Now declutter.

We have all bought kitchen gadgets that we thought would be the answer to our meal prayers and sadly they're not. If there is an item in your kitchen that has not been used in the last six months... it's time to go. Unbeknownst to you, it is renting space in your head. If you have any plastic containers that are separated from their lids; get rid of them too. I want you to get to the stage that there is a place in your kitchen for everything or that every time you look for something in your kitchen, you can simply open a drawer or cupboard and it is smiling out at you.

Getting your kitchen sorted is one of the most productive activities that you can engage in and will have a long-lasting positive effect on your health and wellbeing.

A little note on gadgets: there are kitchen gadgets that I treasure. I miss them every time I cook in someone else's kitchen. Without them, my powers of producing a dish that is delicious and nutritious are severely reduced. I have created a list of my favourite kitchen gadgets which I need to do battle in the kitchen.

Lesson No.3 - Gadgets My Top 10 Gadgets

1. Robert Welch Knife and Sharpener
2. Y shaped Peeler & Y shaped Julienne Peeler
3. Box grater
4. Zyliss Garlic Press
5. Micro plane
6. Lemon Squeezer
7. Salad Spinner
8. Food Tongs
9. Food Bag Clips
10. Pyrex glass dishes with plastic lids

And a cheeky number 11. Omniblend Blender

Lesson No.4 - Online grocery shopping

Lifesaving. Saves time and energy and prevents you from getting seduced into promotions. You reduce the number of decisions you have to make drastically without the marketing strategies that are hard to resist. Initially online shopping takes time but factor in the time it is currently taking you to drive to the supermarket, walk down the aisles, queue at the checkouts, unpack your shopping at the checkout, pay, repack into bags, get to the car, pack all the groceries into the boot, drive home, unload the car. Take it from me; it is much easier to sit down in the comfort of your own kitchen: scroll, click and send.

PS You are aiming to buy 75% of your food online and, of course, you will have to do some grocery shopping during the week, but you have definitely reduced the burden of it. When you have mastered your online shopping challenge, the next step is to create a shopping list that reflects the layout of your kitchen cupboards and fridge shelves. This really speeds up the process, and with the clever 'online shopping' apps that collate the items that you buy most frequently, soon your grocery shopping will be very streamlined.

Lesson No.5 - Instead of Meal Planning, it's Ingredient Prepping.

Prepping your vegetables on the day that you purchase/receive them from the supermarket will revolutionise your meals and help you create the shift. Combine this practice with catching up on missed episodes of your favourite TV shows on catch-up TV, start a box set on Netflix, listen to your favourite music. If you are digitally detoxing at 9pm, use this prep time to your advantage. Buy yourself an assortment of Pyrex glass (not plastic) dishes with plastic lids that you can store your prepped vegs in.

Often the hardest part of getting lunch and dinner ready is the thought of prepping the vegetables. Your salad, vegetable drawer in the fridge may be brimming over with fabulous produce, but because it's in a drawer it may sadly get forgotten; the only winner here is the 'food caddy' when the vegetables have gone past their 'eat by date' and they lie depressed, limp and overlooked and their final destination is the food caddy ready for bin day. We've all done it!

PS I used to think that prepping your vegetables long before you were going to eat them would radically reduce their vitamin and mineral content. That might be the case, but if they are sitting unused in the fridge chiller drawer, no one is getting any value from them. If that all seems a bit like hard work; the supermarkets are only too happy to give us a helping hand. Many of the vegetables today are chopped and readily prepped for us. But have you seen the super inflated price that goes with this convenience? Sometimes this cost is well worth it if you are pushed for time. The freezer section of your supermarket is often overlooked. Vegetables in the frozen section are prepped for you at a more realistic price.

Years ago frozen vegetables equalled frozen garden peas or sweet corn; those days are long gone now. Now there is a magnificent array… spinach, broccoli, aubergines, peppers, diced onions, butternut squash - the list goes on.

Lesson No.6 – Buy yourself ONE good knife.

Personally, I would recommend an 8" knife. Believe me; this will transform your relationship with prepping vegetables. Sharpen often and never, ever put it in the dishwasher. Let no-one put it in the dishwasher. In fact, don't let anyone else touch it. The next step is learning how to use it. Sharpen your knife skills. You can do this in the comfort of your own kitchen. Just jump on YouTube, where there are some fabulous videos to follow on knife skills.

Lesson No.7 – An Injection of Colour, Texture and Flavour

Colour, Texture, Flavour - inject all of these into your meals and you will get the variety your body craves. Colour - this box is already ticked by the array of colours in the vegetable kingdom. A special note on the 'colour green' - you get bonus marks if you include this colour in your diet every single day. Green vegetables contain the most nutrients in the plant kingdom. Flavour - When I first started out on my 'vegetable mission' I had a really good think about the flavours and styles of cuisine that I was attracted to. Think of the restaurants that you would choose on a night out; Thai, Indian, Italian, Chinese, Mexican, Spanish, Greek, Lebanese and think of the particular dishes you would choose and start creating these flavour combinations at home.

My Top Flavours (Herbs and Spices)

1. Cumin Seeds
2. Crushed Chillies
3. Dried Oregano
4. Lemons
5. Limes
6. Salt
7. Black Pepper
8. Garlic
9. Ginger (also available in the frozen aisle)
10. Fresh Coriander (or frozen)
11. Fresh Mint (or frozen)
12. Fresh Parsley (or frozen)
13. Fresh Basil (or frozen)
14. Tamari Sauce
15. Worcestershire Sauce

A combination of raw and cooked vegetables really adds texture and colour to your meals...nuts and seeds are great for this!

Just think about it you can change the texture of a carrot in numerous ways, i.e. dice, chop, grate, ribbon. One of my sons remarked the other day that vegetables taste different depending on the way they are prepped.

Lesson 8 - Keep your kitchen clean.

Always go to bed with a clean sink and kitchen. Always! Even if every other room in the house is upside down; prioritise your kitchen. This, in the end, will add the most value to your life. Having dishes to wash in the morning and possibly having to clear your kitchen takes way longer in the morning, minutes at night convert into a time haemorrhage in the morning and it really zaps your mental energy.

Lesson No.9– Food Made with Love.

I love, love, love cooking, but I do not I love the slog of cooking every night.

My idea of cooking is a chilled-out experience, a glass of wine in my hand, maybe even a G&T, music in the background. After school, weekday meals do not have the same appeal, and the cooking experience described earlier is just not going to happen.

Anything I can do to make weekday meals quicker, easier, still nutritious and delicious sounds good enough to me. I need them stress-free and made with love.

With two boys, it's a necessity to make mealtimes as stress-free as possible, and this is my main priority. Stress prevention is definitely much better than the cure, and I need to pick my battles wisely. A good diet will be of little benefit if we are all stressed. I want them to remember meals times as a pleasurable experience. Of course I would love myself and them to choose the most nutritious option the majority of the time, but there are nights when I come in after picking them up that pizza, fish fingers are extremely appealing, and that's what I serve BUT I always serve them with huge portions of vegetables dosed with added colour, flavour, texture and a little bit of creative flair.

So cooking for the children is not an excuse for me not to manage ticking of my EAT rituals. If anything they are following my lead and they too have a fairly healthy vegetable repertoire for ten-year-olds. Mushrooms though are definitely off the menu. Interestingly the more they see me eat vegetables, the more they are inspired to eat them too.

Food made with love that's what really counts!

I'm curious. Have a think over the last twenty-four hours.

1. How many different vegetables have you eaten?

2. How many different colours of food have you eaten?

3. Have you eaten the colour green?

There are days that I would rather stick pins in my eyes than go out and exercise.

As you have probably guessed, I don't always enjoy the thought of exercising, but I do love the feeling afterwards. And I always have to remind myself of that. I'm sure it's that little squirt of dopamine that gets released within my brain and lights it up like the Las Vegas Strip or the endocannabinoids (marijuana-like substances) that possibly reduce my anxiety. Who knows? All I know is that I feel instantly virtuous after I finish my run or walk whatever exercise I have chosen to do. What about you?

I suspect the characters in the Downstairs Emotional System of my brain have had an opportunity to 'chill out' and Mr PFC is delighted with me because he's had an opportunity to focus and actually see me follow through on a goal that has so many benefits for me long term. My upstairs/downstairs characters are all 'happy' with me. I exercise to keep my brain in shape and not my body. The funny thing is that if your brain's in shape, everything else falls into 'shape'.

Even though I have made the connection between the feelings post-exercise, there are still times when I have to coax myself into getting started. My Emotional System doesn't buy into my long term goals and doesn't want to play ball or any other form of exercise. It's screaming - 'I DON'T FEEL LIKE EXERCISING!! This can mean I can become the queen of making excuses, and the 'I'm busy' card gets flashed. It's then that I employ my 'mini-habit' strategy. I tell myself that on the days that I am going to run or walk that I only have to do it for 2 minutes. Yes, 2 minutes!

Who can't do 2 minutes? After 2 minutes, I am completely free to stop, and I still have achieved success. The truth is I will always keep on going because I have got over that debilitating state of inertia - I have created that golden momentum that gets me over doing nothing. And I've fooled my Emotional System – 2 minutes is all it took. It's my secret weapon, and it always works.

I am so glad I listened in those physics lessons - I knew Newton's First Law of Motion would come in handy 'A body will stay at rest unless you give it darn good reason to get moving' adapted by me for 21st-century living!!

The way I see it the benefits of exercise are enormous, and we either have to do it, OR we are caught up thinking about doing it, OR we are feeling guilty about not doing it.

You cannot ignore the benefits. Every magazine you open, every tabloid, it's somewhere lurking in your Facebook posts, Instagram, Twitter feeds. Someone somewhere is shouting about the benefits of exercise. And it's all true! And your MR.PFC is listening!

So far in my lifetime, I have completed a few 5km Race for Life runs, a couple of 10kms, hired a personal trainer, tried Pilates and Zumba (I am just not coordinated enough), and attended a circuit class. I'm sure I have tried aerobics too (the thing is, I can't tell the difference between my left and my right, so I am a 'health and safety hazard' at these classes). I have played tennis and squash, joined a running club, and my daily movement is to walk. Of all of these, here are the ones I have enjoyed the most - Couch to 5k, training with a friend, tennis and squash, circuit classes, the ladies running club, and walking, walking, walking, walking.

Upon reflection, morning is my best time to exercise. After midday, there is little hope of it happening, and I have that niggling recurring energy-depleting thought of 'I should exercise' following me around.

The earlier I get it pencilled in, the more mental energy I know I am conserving for, the more life-enhancing decisions and possibly the doses of willpower I might need later on in the day.

Research has also shown that you get a 12-hour mood-boosting effect from exercising in the morning and especially if it is outdoors. That keeps Madam Hypothalamus running like clockwork with all that glorious daylight.

Before really focusing on making every day count, I suffered from the intensity bug; surely, I had to feel some sort of pain to make it worthwhile? I had to be lifting weights, exercising at full pelt for at least an hour, running further and faster. Forget that…consistency and commitment are key.

Couch to 5k - I loved the training possibly because I did it with a friend, and there was a specific target; we completed the Race for Life run together. But somewhere in my head, once I had completed the race, unpinned my race number and put away my medal, that particular box was ticked. Once the challenge had been met, the bubble had burst. I just couldn't keep the running going for some reason.

Squash and tennis I love, but coordinating diaries etc. with friends proved impossible. Aerobics, circuits and similar exercise classes....I always begrudge the lag time between leaving home and getting to the venue. It was never forty-five mins, the advertised length of the class. I had to change my clothes, drive there, and add in a few more distractions so all in all it took well over an hour.

Anything that gets in the way of exercising WILL! I call them 'Points of Resistance'.

I have two rules for exercise:-

KISS - 'Keep it sweet and simple' or as my husband says 'Keep it stupid and simple'. This reduces the number of opportunities to resist, in other words, ' excuses' that I can come up with, that prevent me from getting started on any chosen exercise.

Can I do this when I am 80? So after dabbling for years in various types of exercise, I have done enough experimenting. The trick as you have probably read time and time again is to find something you like to do because these are the only forms of exercise you can insert with confidence so that you really 'Make Every Day Count.'

Success to me is not beating personal best times; it's a fact I am actually doing the exercise at all.

I now know without a shadow of a doubt I love walking (the most), and I like running (up to 4km by myself). I also like running in a group once a week. Group running ticks the box for both exercise and connection. I also love being out in nature. The park is my gym. I have resigned myself to the fact that I am not training for the Olympics. There is no need to represent my town, my county, my country, in any discipline I choose to follow.

After having twins, it is unlikely that I will ever have a six-pack.

This is what I do. 30 minutes + 7 minutes - that's it. That's the time in my day I have allocated to exercise. If you are going to do it daily, then that's more than enough — consistency over intensity.

My allocated 30 minutes for aerobic exercise is outdoors, twice a week I run, and the other days I include brisk walking. It's the same route (3.75km), so I don't have to faff making decisions. I build variety in by running on two days and walking on the others. I always use an app to log the run so I can get a satisfying, job well-done dose of serotonin when I look back at my progress. I can miss one day but never 2....!

At the moment I walk briskly seven days a week because we have a new puppy, but when she's ready, I will introduce her too to the benefits of running twice a week.

Seven minutes - Strength Training. It's important. We steadily lose muscle mass after thirty-five. I don't want to wake one day and not be able to do the things I take for granted; lifting, pushing, pulling... etc. We don't always appreciate things until we lose them. Muscle soaks up sugar (glucose) like a sponge. The secret to longevity and ageing well is balancing your blood sugars. When your blood sugars behave like they are on a roller coaster, this can lead to unlimited inflammation within the body - the root cause I believe of many of our degenerative diseases that are steadily on the increase.

I use the Full Body workout – '7' App on my smartphone. I complete one loop. It consists of thirty seconds of each of the following exercises; jumping jacks, wall sits, push-ups, crunches, step-ups, squats, triceps dips, plank, high knees, running in place, lunges, push-ups with rotation and side plank with a ten-second rest between. I give it my all, and it's over in seven-minute fifty-three secs. Oops...I lied about the seven mins! Seven minutes sounds so much better than eight and seven is my favourite number.

I am sure you have covered many of these exercises if you have attended classes at a gym or had a personal trainer. I started where I was at, with zero judgements and built on it. For example, I could only manage a press-up using my knees. I kept challenging myself, and now I can do a fairly decent press up, even the boys are impressed.

The boys will join me and believe it, or not hubby does it too with me.

It's actually good fun. I add variety by challenging myself to add one more repetition of each exercise within the allocated timeframe each week to push myself out of my comfort zone.

My advice is to start where you are at, apply no judgement, tell yourself you are great and make incremental improvements.

Ohh and I nearly forgot; I can wear my normal clothes to do this. Points of resistance reduced. I do use a good deodorant....I hope!

Exercise is only part of the much bigger Health Pillar - Move.

We were designed to MOVE and to move frequently throughout the day. Even the guidelines from the Department of Health recommend minimising the amount of time spent being sedentary (sitting) for extended periods. I'm impressed. Lots of us fall into the category of Active - Sedentary. Yes, we do exercise a few times a week but for the remainder of our day (apart from sleeping in our beds) we spend it sitting; in the car or train to work, at work, at our TV or computer at night.

Most of us spend as much as 55% or more of our waking hours each day sitting.

A growing number of studies show that the more we sit, the greater the chances of dying of heart disease, stroke, cancer or diabetes. Sitting also saps our energy making us more tired than normal. Why does this happen? Sit too much, and we experience the same types of negative effects that astronauts experience in the microgravity of outer space. By sitting too much, we are reducing the effect of gravity here on earth. We can't 'exercise' our way out of sitting too much. We need to take regular breaks from sitting by getting up, standing and moving your body.

Joan Vernikos served as a Life Science Director at the NASA Research Centre. In her book Sitting Kills, Moving Heals she writes: "The physical deterioration suffered by astronauts in space in a matter of days, mirrors what happens to all of us here on earth as we age. However, living in space profoundly magnifies the changes that normally take a lifetime to appear. On earth from the age of 20, we lose roughly 1.6 per cent of our bone density a year. Astronauts in space, on average, lose 1.6 per cent of their bone density per month, and some have lost as much as 1 per cent in a single week! This is on top of their muscles becoming weaker, their immune systems being suppressed, and their sleep being disturbed. And when they first return from space, they have less stamina, they shuffle when walking, and they have lost their sense of balance. It's tough being an Astronaut!"

The reason Astronauts lose their strength and vitality is that they no longer get pushed on by gravity. When we sit for extended periods, it's as if we're are living in outer space. The solution is to make sure we get up and move around at least every thirty minutes even if we exercise regularly, increase our opportunities to move even a little, frequently throughout the day. That's why I use my Fitbit. I aim for 10,000 steps, and on most days, I pass this. I am not married to 10,000 steps. I am more interested in making sure that I have moved continually throughout the day. There is also a little alarm on the Fitbit to remind you to move every hour, and you can play around with that.

MINDSET MATTERS......Why thinking you got a work out may actually make you healthier!

I still skip for joy for stumbling upon this research. It's one of those nuggets of information you find when you are going down the Google' rabbit hole.'

Harvard University psychologist Ellen Langer and her student Alia Crum found that many of the beneficial results of exercise are due to the placebo effect. They carried out a study that involved hotel housekeepers. According to the study, many housekeepers did not perceive their job as exercise, but what if their mindset was shifted so that they became aware of the exercise they were getting, then what health improvements would follow.

The researchers studied eighty-four female housekeepers from seven hotels.

Women in four hotels were told that their regular work was enough exercise to meet the requirements for a healthy, active lifestyle, whereas the women in the other three hotels were told nothing. To determine if the placebo effect plays a role in the benefits of exercise, the researchers investigated whether subjects' mindset (in this case, their perceived levels of exercise) could inhibit or enhance the health benefits of exercise independent of any actual exercise.

Four weeks later, the researchers returned to assess any changes in women's health. They found that the women in the informed group had lost an average of 2 pounds, lowered their blood pressure by almost 10 per cent, and were significantly healthier as measured by body-fat percentage, body mass index, and waist-to-hip ratio. These changes were significantly higher than those reported in the control group and were especially remarkable given the time period of only four weeks.

Langer writes, "Whether the change in physiological health was brought about directly or indirectly, it is clear that health is significantly affected by mindset." This research shows the moderating role of mindset and its ability to enhance health, which may have particular relevance for treating diseases associated with a sedentary lifestyle.

I have adapted this piece of research into my life and my exercise regimen. My move rituals include 7 minutes of strength training, walking briskly for 30 minutes a day and generally moving throughout the day at regular intervals. The brisk walking does not have to be done in one stretch. I have made it that easy for myself that I can do it in three x 10-minute stints or any other combination.

A few years ago, I would have laughed out loud at this exercise regime; I had mistakenly thought I needed to be much tougher on myself. There were many days back then that I had failed to tick the 'exercise box' and that indirectly would have affected other decisions I made in my life. Not any more, I can quite easily achieve the exercise targets I describe above. There is no longer any head chatter about joining a gym, going to a class, etc. My mindset has changed, and consequently, my exercise has reduced, more to the point I can now consistently do it daily and feel successful.

The only caveat I have is that from time to time in the future I will re-join the running group in my local town. I have done that in the past and thoroughly enjoyed it. The reason I do this is because of the connection and camaraderie with the other runners; it's a ladies running group, and it's not solely to exercise. The quality of conversation when you are running together is so enriching. The same applies when my neighbour rings me up on the spur of the moment, and we are luckily in a position to go for a run together. I'm not sure if it's the tempo of the run, but I always come away from our conversations inspired and energised.

Over to you…

Have a look at your exercise history; what form of exercise could you do daily that you truthfully enjoyed over the years?

Can you imagine yourself doing it when you are 80?

What excuses get in your way?

When the To-Do list is finally ticked off; then and only then will I rest!

In the past, this was my attitude to REST and RELAXATION. Let's face it being a Mum, running my own business with a hubby that travelled a lot; I had no relationship with rest. Getting everything ticked off the To-Do list just never happened. There was no time left....after the To-Doing bit, to do the To-Being bit and REST.

In my head, REST or any form of relaxation was a luxury only available to the highly productive and efficient. Not me! It was something you deserved. There was never enough time in my schedule to fit it in. Squeezing it in would be a step too far and if anything added to my stress. Bottom line it was not top of my priorities and it definitely never qualified to get a space on any well-intentioned list.

For you, it may not be seen as a luxury but a sign of weakness. I understood the prehistoric response to stress that has been hard-wired into our brain with its biological and biochemical effects on our body in depth. It has helped us 'Fight-Flight or Freeze' in some very compromising scenarios down through the centuries by producing cortisol.

Cortisol, the body's main stress hormone is like a high octane fuel. Once released, it quickly prioritises the bodily functions and resources that are essential for our survival.

It down-regulates the activities in the body that are not required in that particular moment to keep us alive such as digestion. In modern times we are unlikely to encounter sabre-toothed tigers; in reality, we are attacked by modern-day life itself.

In my teenage years, stress symbolised the overweight, middle-aged businessman clutching his heart in the throes of a heart attack, and because I would never fit into that category, it never concerned me.

In my 20s, the busy days still had time for relaxation. The digital era had not exploded. We had the luxury of no internet, no mobile phones. We had landlines and five channels on the TV. I may not have used it wisely, but there was time.

By my late 30's and as a result of passing years; children and ageing parents in another country, stress came knocking on the door. All of us can identify these big stressors; children, elderly parents, critical illness and the death of loved ones. But it's the low-grade everyday stress; the morning routine with the children that never goes to plan, the rugby boots that have gone missing, the dog that has eaten the homework, work deadline looming, yet another set of road works, train cancellations and the boys are going to be late for the umpteenth time this term, for school and work; the list goes on.

These daily stressors come relentlessly and are our modern-day 'sabre-toothed tigers'. Our brain cannot distinguish between the big life stressors and the daily irritations that when strung together become the big life stressors and have the same damaging effect on our bodies.

For someone that prided herself and awarded myself a badge of honour for remaining calm in the face of stress and adversity; I was fooling myself. No one is immune to the effects of stress. Stress is ubiquitous. It's everywhere and part and parcel of 21st Century living. I finally blew my limiting belief that REST was a luxury when I got to grips with the workings of my brain.

Success to me is when I'm there for my children and husband and also my happy place. That is when I am making progress in my life; achieving my goals/projects, connected with my family and friends, and dedicated to self-care. This needs a tremendous amount of focus and planning.

Focus and planning come about when there is a collaboration between the characters of my downstairs (my emotional brain): Sergeant Major Amygdala, Party Animal Nucleus Accumbens, Director of Status Quo Madame Hypothalamus and Ole Captain Basal Ganglia and Mr PFC - the main character of my upstairs (my thinking brain). Stress completely shuts down any communication between the two levels. Resting is like giving the downstairs characters a little daily 'Spa' experience' so that they work with Mr PFC for my greater good. This is especially important for Sergeant Major Amygdala who can get his 'Long Johns' in a right old twist. If he's happy, Madame Status Quo is happy and restrains herself from continually squeezing her finger on the 'flight/fight switch' - our sympathetic nervous system thus reducing our exposure to the damaging effects of cortisol. When both of them are sorted there is less need for our 'bad habits' to surface from deep within our Basal Ganglia, and our Party animal is less likely to seek out its next big hit of dopamine.

With rest, the order is restored, survival is ensured; then and only then can Mr PFC get on with the important business of planning a brighter future and by using willpower wisely I ensure the choices I make on a daily basis are helping me thrive. The 'spa experience' for my downstairs characters can be as little as one minute per day to start with. And there is the perfect spa experience provided by Mother Nature, free and available anytime; to breathe.

Paying attention to your breath without judgement of any undisciplined thoughts that wander in and out of your mind is exactly what the downstairs characters crave for serenity. This spa practice may also resemble meditation, but I have always struggled with developing a meditation practice - twenty/thirty minutes seemed far too long for me. Taking a breather for one minute or five or even ten minutes just seemed a doable amount for me, and in this situation, I apply the 'Goldilocks Effect' - not too much, not too little, just the right amount. Concentrating on your breathing will very quickly pull you out of our 'flight, fight or freeze' response and switch on your' rest and digest' system.

It is worth noting that we can only last about three minutes without breathing. Is that not a tell-tale sign of its significance, maybe? So we cannot eat or drink our way out of stress, but how many of us do try this approach? Thankfully, we can breathe our way out of stress.

Lots of our stress is induced by our ability to time travel in our mind. We live in the past plagued by regret and guilt and live in the future with fear, worry and anxiety.

Very few live in the present moment unless we consciously commit. Concentrating on your breath is the fastest way of bringing you into the present. Give it a try, if only for a minute.

As for Mr PFC, by sheer default gains the benefits of the spa experience for the downstairs characters. His unique 'Resting' experience takes the form of decluttering, mentally and physically. Mentally - this is addressed by reducing the number of daily decisions that you make so you do not suffer the effects of 'decision fatigue'. Physically, it's that clutter in your homes and workspace - another source of mental fatigue. You have no idea until you start this process how much cerebral energy you will preserve and regenerate when you start to 'declutter'. This energy can then be used for powering up your 'Willpower'.

Breathing and decluttering are not the only forms of rest available. In a society that encourages overwork too, science now shows us that we can all work better, be more productive, and have happier lives if we learn how to balance work and rest.

Alex Pang writes in his book 'Rest' that work and rest need to partner with each other and not be seen as opposites. In life, we are very well versed in the 'work' bit of the partnership, possibly educated through mainstream education, college, and university or entered into an apprenticeship or work experience. If you pause to think; work has gone from a nine to five activity to filling every available hour. We can carry our office around in our pocket by means of a mobile phone and just because we can check our emails at any time it has turned into a commandment that we must.

If you think about it, very few of us have learned the skill of resting. By default, we have zoned or numbed out in front of the TV and think we are ticking the rest box. Not so! We need to detach from the 'work' part of our life by switching off from our digital devices and move away from the concept that we can work anywhere, anytime, anyplace. Resting from work is of vital importance to our wellbeing.

Elite sporting professionals and some of the most ambitious, successful people on the planet now take rest seriously. There is prolific research on the benefits of naps, and personally, I am thrilled! For me, it's the quickest way of shutting down my overwrought emotional limbic system and my thinking brain. My mother does it, my grandmother did it, and my great grandmother did it. With this scientific approval, I now do it without guilt. I design my day that although I get up really early, I can have a nap if I need to.

Winston Churchill did it. He proclaimed that it was like having two days for the price of one. Many of the top sports professionals take naps before their sporting events to aid performance. Creative people tend to design their days by getting up early and take deliberate rest in the form of a nap, run, swim or walk where their minds can wander, and often they come up with a subconscious solution to their creative project. Rest makes people more creative than reactive. There is also a natural rhythm to nature. Night follows the day and then we have the seasons. Our bodies follow a circadian rhythm too, a twenty-four hour period where our hormones are finely tuned to the day/night cycle, that's if we respect it.

According to Tony Schwarz, co-author of "The Power of Full Engagement' our bodies also follow what is known as ultradian rhythms - ninety-minute periods, at the end of which we reach the limits of our capacity to work at the highest level. It is possible to push ourselves past ninety minutes by relying on coffee, or sugar, or by summoning up our stress hormones, but when we do this, we are overriding our physiological need for intermittent rest and renewal. Eventually, there's a price to pay. The suggestion is that no matter what particular form of work you are involved in focusing intently for ninety minutes followed by a twenty-minute break is the way forward. This 'powers up' your productivity. I have adjusted this slightly to forty-five minutes highly focused time blocks followed by ten minutes of some other activity that doesn't need focus.

When I experimented with time blocks, I found forty-five minutes worked much better for me. I am unsure of the reason. I think moving away from the idea that you can sit down and work for hours and hours is just not doable. Personally, I can only be productive when I break down my day in time blocks as opposed to looking at one long stretch of time. That seems to de-energise me from the start. I need something to look forward to. By allowing myself to focus for forty-five minutes at a time, those mini-breaks never seem far away. They are my reward!

If you use the ninety-minute time block, you have three focused blocks a day. That's all you can manage. That equates to four and a half hours. We fool ourselves into thinking we can be productive for eight hours a day. If you are inspired by this idea of resting, then it actually gives you permission to switch off from work at the end of the day. You are spent, you've worked hard, and now it's time to rest in earnest.

It is important to remember to make sure one of these time blocks is used within the 8 am - 11 am slot where our energy is at its peak, and you are most creative. Use it wisely by not checking emails or by someone else hijacking your precious time.

I want to leave you with a thought. If you unscrambled the letters of the word STRESS and dropped a couple of the S's, you would come up with the word REST -the perfect antidote to stress.

There are some fantastic Meditation Apps on the market. I use the Calm App, and I feel like Tamara Levitt is part of the family now. She writes and narrates the meditation sessions. On a daily basis, she leaves you with some wonderful insights. I'd miss her if I didn't spend time with her every day.

Rest more. Accomplish more. Have you dedicated any time to 'Rest' today?

My Top Daily Habits

1. Asleep by 10.30pm every night
2. Digital Shutdown at 9pm
3. Walk every day - 30 mins
4. Strength training ~7 minutes each day (7 App)
5. Breakfast, Lunch and Dinner. No Snacks
6. Vegetables - 50% of my daily food intake
7. Drink four glasses of water daily
8. Breathing/ Meditation -10 mins
9. Gratitude Practice; 3 things each night
10. Declutter for 15 minutes per day
11. Journal; What's on My Mind? - 10mins

My PS Ritual. I have thought long and hard about including this, my final ritual, into my book…..

12. Remembering daily those that have added value and continue to add value to my life

It has been part of my day since my birthday in November 2017, and it is very much part of my life now because it gives me peace. I started it as a way of dealing with the overwhelming grief I feel when I think of my Dad.

My Dad, as I have written before, is in the late stages of dementia and last summer the family had to make that painful decision of moving him to a nursing home close to our family home. By the time my birthday came around my Dad no longer knew me and I think because of my circumstances (I live in England, and my family home is in Northern Ireland) I was the first of his children that he didn't recognise. Heart breaking.

As far back as I can remember whenever I had to deal with anything too painful; my strategy was that if it was out of sight, it was out of my mind.

That's how I cope.

I never want my Dad to be out of my mind, but in those early months, after he went into the nursing home whenever I did think of him, I was consumed by grief. Dementia is like a thief; it comes and steals the person from you and then you have to endure what feels like the long goodbye. What I know for having spent a lifetime with my Dad; no way would he want anyone to spend their days grieving for him. I have many wonderful, cherished memories of him and that's what I hold on to now.

He just had the best smile, and his eyes always lit up, that has faded now. Another great memory was that whenever you asked him how he was doing, he would always reply "I'm powerful" and from where I'm from that means 'I am doing just great.' There was no half-hearted reply - 'not bad'; it was always 'I'm powerful'.

So every day now at the beginning of my day I bless his day and remember how 'powerful' he was and I'm sure still is. I actually write the words down because that really signifies to me that I have actually taken the moments and remembered him in my day.

As I said earlier, I started this in November, and as the months passed, I added to this practice. I now also take the time to remember the people that mean most in my life, my family and friends and I bless their day because they add so much to my days and my life.

There are three prayers that come at the end of my journal practice.

The Serenity Prayer
God grant me the serenity to accept the things I cannot change, the courage to change the things I can, and wisdom to know the difference.

Prayer of St. Francis of Assisi
Lord, make me an instrument of thy peace.
Where there is hatred, let me sow love;
Where there is injury, pardon;
Where there is doubt, faith;
Where there is despair, hope;
Where there is darkness, light;
Where there is sadness, joy
O divine Master, grant that I may not so much to seek
To be consoled as to console,
To be understood as to understand,
To be loved as to love;
For it is in giving that we receive;
It is in pardoning that we are pardoned;
It is dying to self that we are born to eternal life.

I am not sure where I found this prayer, but I include it every day.

May I be happy, may I be safe, may I be healthy and may I be at peace.

Thank you. Nora

Once we understand the steps to forming habits; we have one very useful strategy for creating significant changes in our lives. Getting into the habit of habits is the 'Holy Grail' of health and wellbeing. Knowledge has potential but no power without habitual action. The space between Knowledge and Doing is furnished with habits. Making Every Day Count begins and ends with a set of value-adding habits. Did I mention the word Habit?

Let's get started……

Consider specific times during your day.

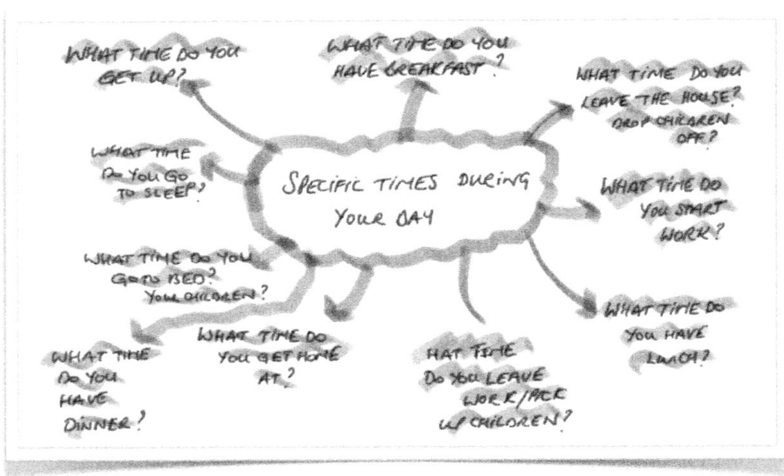

Complete the time slots on the template over the page.

TIME	OBLIGATIONS	CUE	TINY HABIT
6.00AM			
7.00AM			
8.00AM			
9.00AM			
10.00AM			
11.00AM			
12.00PM			
1.00PM			
2.00PM			
3.00PM			
4.00PM			
5.00PM			
6.00PM			
7.00PM			
8.00PM			
9.00PM	DIGITAL SHUTDOWN		DIGITAL SHUTDOWN
10.00PM			
10.30PM	ASLEEP	ASLEEP	ASLEEP

Pick your Habit

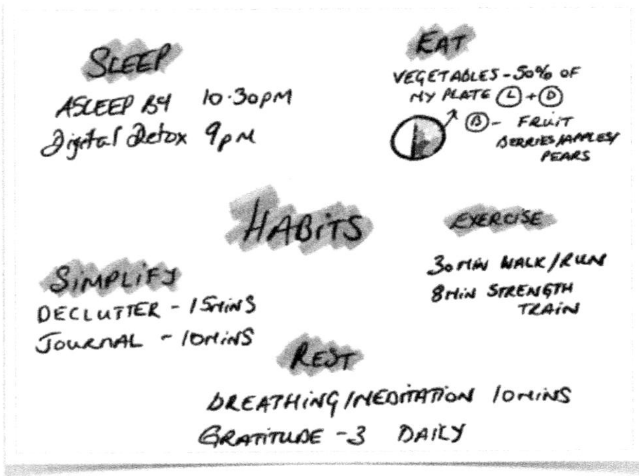

Then Loop the Loop of the Habit Loop

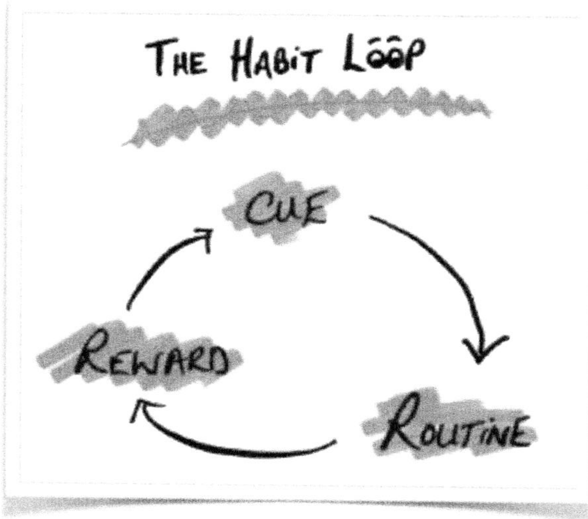

Search for Obvious Cues throughout Your Day.... Look for cues during your day that your brain has to mentally trip over and list them. You will come back to this list again and again.

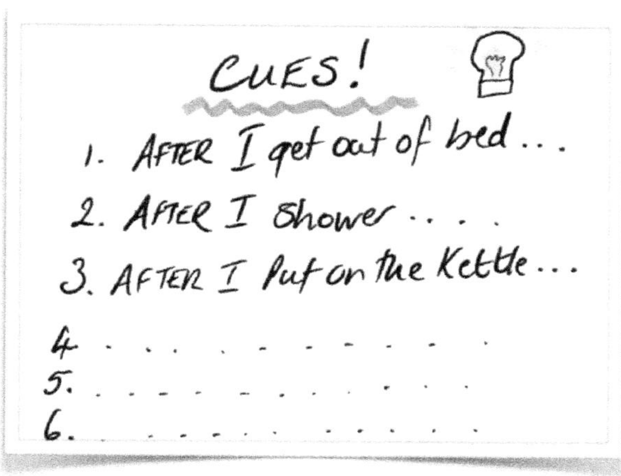

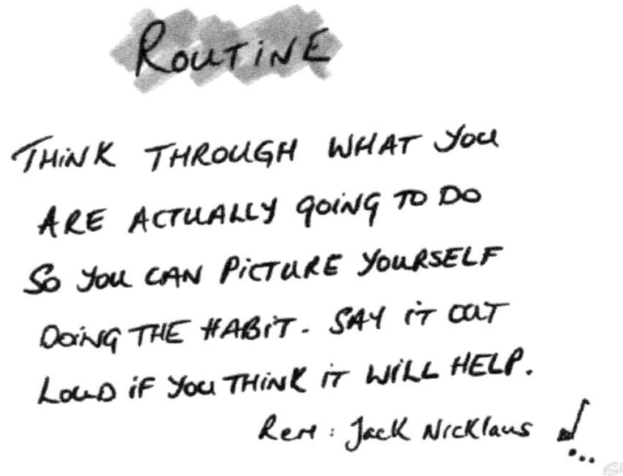

Plan for Failure

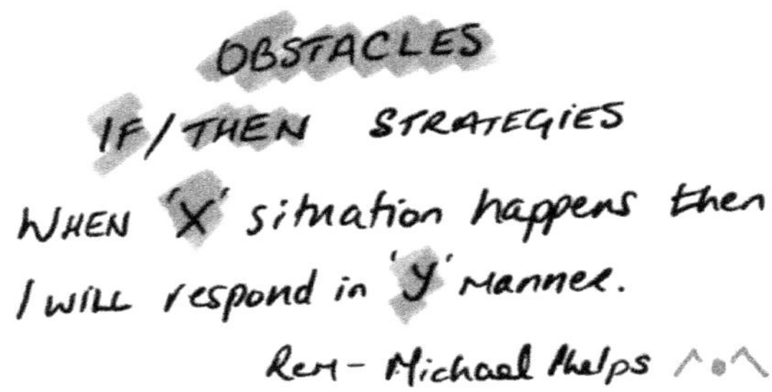

Reward Yourself

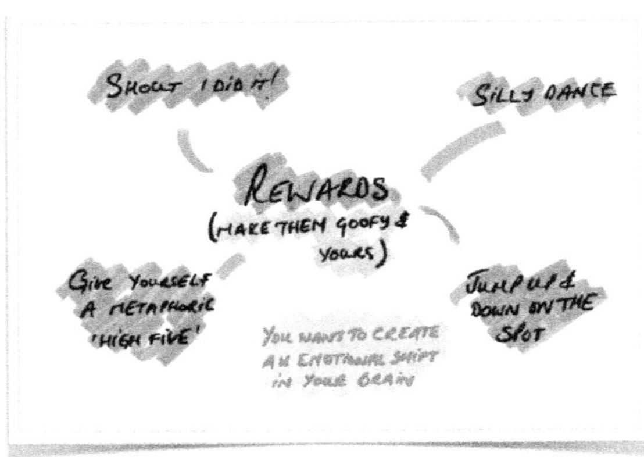

Track your Habits and Remind Yourself of your Why?

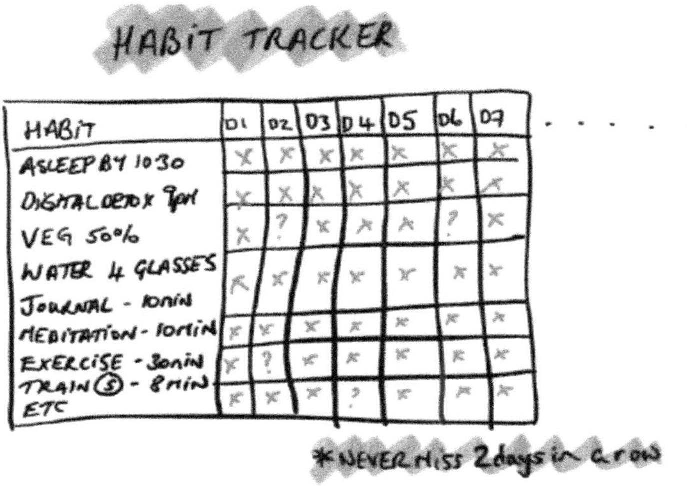

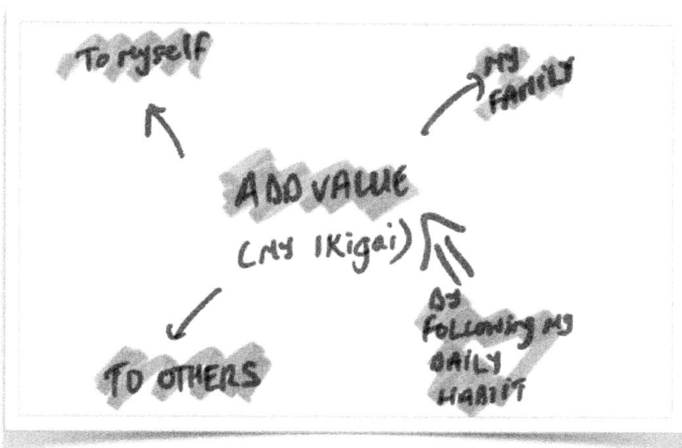

Grow that Mind Set - Learning Opportunities

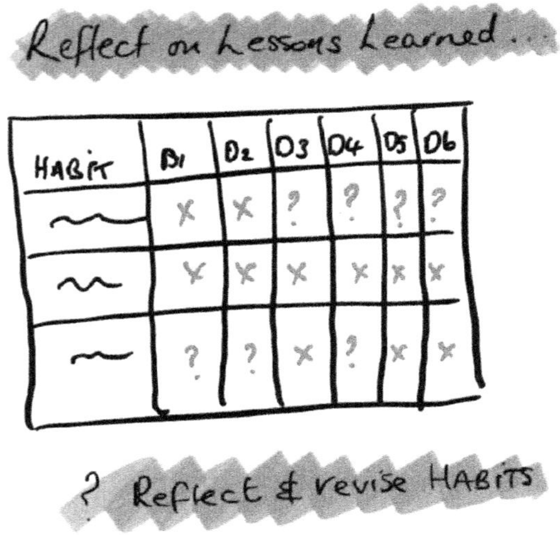

The Personal Challenge - Fast Track Habits

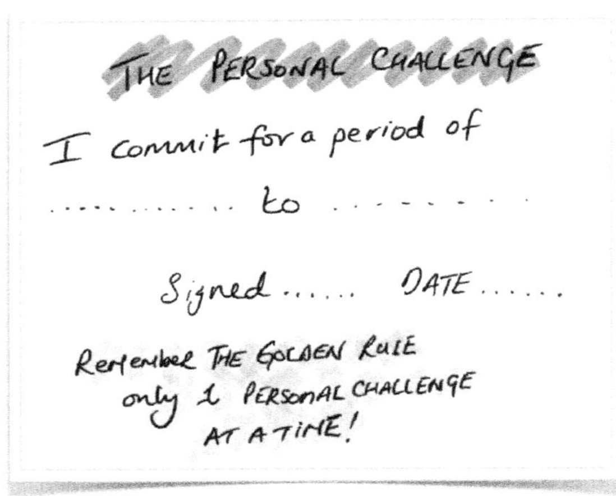

Lessons Learned…

A-HA! MOMENTS.

LESSONS LEARNED

1.

2.

3.

The last few words from me...

I have written this book as much for myself as for you. So thank you.

I hope you have enjoyed it and that I have offered a simpler and easier approach to some of the changes you have been trying to make in your life. Little changes in the right direction, however small when added together are very powerful. Start with one tiny habit.

I hope you have found at least one nugget of wisdom that will brighten the spark within.

I hope it has quietened some of those annoying 'shoulds' in your head and that tiresome inner critic that dwells in all our heads and in so doing has settled your head.

And I hope this book has inspired you to step out of your comfort zone, embracing a growth mindset to become the expert on you.

In a world full of information, you still need to ask questions, but maybe in the not too distant future, you will be asking a different set of questions because you have the basics already covered.

My wish for you is that for those times that adversity comes knocking on your door, you will have created a set of habits for each of your days that give you resilience and strength. It is much better to 'be ready, than get ready' and may you gain comfort that you live your life; Making Every Day Count.

My wish for you is that: You may be happy, you may be safe, you may be healthy, you may be at peace and may you live making every day count.

Nora x

Resources

One of my core values is to learn something new each day. I read or listen to at least two books a month; sometimes it's a lot more. I have been lucky to stumble across a lot of the books listed below, and the authors have done a fantastic job of getting their ideas into the world, and I want to acknowledge that. I love finding out and experimenting with some nugget of information that will perhaps add value to my life and in turn, hopefully, yours.

I have come to realise that books are my equivalent of designer handbags or clothes. I get a tingle of excitement when I pick up a book, open my kindle or click into my Audible App. Probably sounds a bit nerdy but it's true. Listening to audiobooks has revolutionised my life. I can convert very mundane tasks into something to get excited about just by plugging my earphones in. Below you will find a list of books, video clips; websites that have really helped me join the dots and have inspired me to create daily habits that help me make every day count. I have chosen those books that I feel made the biggest impact on me. I still reread and relisten to most of these books and videos and will continually revisit them. I always pick up something new or understand some of the concepts just a little bit more when I do. I want to share these resources for any of you that want to dig a bit deeper into any of the ideas I have shared so that you can start to connect your own dots. I have also included links to videos where I have been able to; that summarise the main points of many of the books I have read.

Here are some of the resources that I have listened to, watched or read more than once and will relisten, rewatch and reread again.

By way of Introduction

Eat, Move, Sleep – Tom Rath

Know Thyself

The 16 personalities Test (127 million people have taken this test, maybe you have already done it, and I was late to the party) www.16personalities.com

Values

'The Core Values Workbook' - is incredible and FREE at www.dawnbarclay.com

Gretchen Rubin's Quiz: The Four Tendencies www.surveygizmo.com/s3/4232520/gretchenrubinfourtendenciesquiz

The Four Tendancies: The Indispensable Personality Profiles That Reveal How to Make Your Life Better by Gretchen Rubin

Quiet: The Power of Introverts in a World That Can't Stop Talking by Susan Cain

TED talk 'The Power of Introverts www.ted.com/talks/susan_cain_the_power_of_introverts

Legacy

Paper: The future of the NHS the Lancet Published: April 15 https://www.thelancet.com/journals/lancet/article/PIIS0140-6736 (17)30994-7/fulltext

The Key to Success: My Understanding of How the brain works

Mindsight: Transform Your Brain with the New Science of Kindness by Daniel Siegel

Rethinking Positive Thinking, Inside the new science of Motivation by Gabriele Oettingen

The Upward Spiral by Alex Korb

The Whole Brain Child by Dr Tina Payne Bryson and Dr Daniel Siegel

The Chimp Brain Paradox by Prof Steve Peters

Mind Hacking by John Hargrave

Resilient By Rick Hanson

The Willpower Instinct by Kelly McGonigal

Dr Sarah McKay's website yourbrainhealth.com.au

Making Every Day Count - Understanding Habits

The Power of Habit by Charles Duhigg

BJ Fogg at TEDxFremont: Forget big change, start with a tiny habit

https://youtu.be/AdKUJxjn-R8

Atomic Habits: James Clear

Better than Before by Gretchen Rubin

Mini Habits by Stephen Guise.

Box of crayons habit series of videos - very funny!

https://boxofcrayons.com/the-coaching-habit-book/the-coaching-habit-videos/

Mindset by Carol Dweck,

My Why - Carpe Diem?

The Blue Zones

https://www.nationalgeographic.com/books/features/5-blue-zones-where-theworlds-healthiest-people-live/

https://www.bluezones.com

Sleep

Sleep Smarter: 21 Essential Strategies to Sleep Your Way to a Better Body, Better

Health and Bigger Success (2016) by Shawn Stevenson

The Sleep Revolution: Transforming Your Life, One night at a Time (2017) by

Arianna Huffington

Shawn Stevenson: "Sleep Smarter" Talks at Google

Ted Talk: Arianna Huffington, How to succeed; Get more sleep. The Sleep Council

Lucia of Best You Coaching, www.luciabrowne.com

Simplifying

5 Reasons Why We Need a Digital Detox Anthony Ongaro

Digital Minimalism Choosing a Focused Life in a Noisy World by Cal Newport

The Life-Changing Magic of Tidying: A simple, effective way to banish clutter forever

(2014) by Marie Kondo

Video: Tidy Up Your Home: The KonMari Method: Storing clothes

Gratitude

Video: The Science of Gratitude,

YouTube https://youtu.be/JMd1CcGZYwU

Eat

Food Rules: An Eater's Manuel (2010) by Michael Pollan

The Dissident Diet by Dawn Waldron

Foodist: Using Real Food and Real Science to Lose Weight Without Dieting (2015) by Darya Pino Rose

The Thin Woman's Brain by Dilia Suriel

Bright Line Eating by Susan Peirce Thompson

Eat to Live Joel Fuhrman

Eating Tips

Pinterest and www.kitchn.com are fabulous resources for topping up your inspiration in the kitchen. I also use the resource section of Jess Dangs' website www.cooksmarts.com. It has some excellent infograms which I revisit time and time again.

Jules Clancy and her website thestonesoup.com - Jules has a no-nonsense approach to food, menu planning and all things edible. She has a wonderful website full of valuable foodie information.

Movement & Exercise

Michael Mosley: 'Forget walking 10,000 steps a day' By Michael Mosley, BBC https://www.bbc.co.uk/news/health-42864061

To start doing some Active 10s in your day, go to the NHS website where you can download a free Public Health England app. It is a good way to see how much walking you are doing and how to do more. Wear a Fitbit

Strength Training

App - Seven - 7-minute Workout

Mindset Matters: Exercise and the Placebo Effect.Crum, Alia J., and Ellen J.Langer. 2007. Psychological Science 18, no. 2: 165-171.

Sitting Kills, Moving Heals: How Everyday Movement Will Prevent Pain, Illness & Early Death - - & Exercise Alone Won't by Joan Vernikos

Rest

Rest by Alex Soojung-Kim Pang

The Power of Full Engagement by Jim Loehr and Tony Schwarz

Calm App – Fabulous

Meditation 101: How to Meditate without Moving to the Himalayas https://youtu.be/VBb0y5Ck838

Subscriptions

I subscribe monthly to 'Optimise' - an app and website created by Brian Johnson and his team. Each morning you receive a daily dose of wisdom. I have to admit I am heavily influenced by what I hear on a daily basis.

Calm App available on the App store

7 App available on the App store

Fitbit App available on the App Store

Printed in Great
Britain
by Amazon

31206642R00098